Praise for *The Power-Based Life*

"Proverbs 23:7 says, "For as he thinks in his heart, so is he." How many of us have wished we could conquer our fears; overcome bad habits; right the wrongs of our past; achieve our dreams; in short, become the men and women God intended us to be? We can, says Coach Flynt, but the process requires a shift in focus, a mental preparedness that allows us to face any obstacle from a position of power, not weakness. Let Coach Flynt show you how! With his years of experience as a strength-training coach, his incredible life story, and his wealth of spiritual wisdom, he has the credentials to "power-up" your body, mind, and spirit for the challenges life brings. As a psychiatrist and professor, I know I will continue to share the power-based principles in this book with my clients and students for years to come. Thank you, Mike, for sharing your life story with all of us!"

—DAVID LIVINGSTONE HENDERSON, MD;
COAUTHOR, *FINDING PURPOSE BEYOND OUR PAIN*;
HOPE FOR THE HEART CHAIR OF BIBLICAL COUNSELING,
CRISWELL COLLEGE; AND ADJUNCT PROFESSOR
OF BIBLICAL COUNSELING, DALLAS THEOLOGICAL SEMINARY

"Mike Flynt has written a life-changing book! *The Power-Based Life* is loaded with profound wisdom and inspired principles that I believe can benefit people of any age and in all walks of life. Mike uses humor, compassion, and personal experience to challenge and encourage readers. I highly recommend this book for anyone who has ever had a dream and who truly desires to live up to his full potential."

—RICK BOWLES, EXECUTIVE DIRECTOR,
GREATER DALLAS FELLOWSHIP OF CHRISTIAN ATHLETES

"Mike Flynt's life and the lessons shared in *The Power-Based Life* are an inspiration to us all. It has been an honor to know, work with, and learn from Mike. I know that readers of this powerful new book will feel the genuine passion with which he lives."

—[ ] AN FOR LIFE

"Coach Mike Flynt is an inspiratic [ ] n have set an example that can benefit people [ ] *Power-Based Life* is a great read for anyone who wants to improve his body, mind, and spirit."

—BOYD EPLEY, FOUNDER, NATIONAL STRENGTH
AND CONDITIONING ASSOCIATION

THE
POWER
BASED
LIFE

. . . .

THE
POWER
BASED
LIFE

· · · · · · · · · · · · · · · · · · · ·

REALIZE YOUR LIFE'S GOALS AND DREAMS
BY STRENGTHENING YOUR BODY, MIND, AND SPIRIT

MIKE FLYNT

THOMAS NELSON

Since 1798

NASHVILLE   DALLAS   MEXICO CITY   RIO DE JANEIRO

Published in Nashville, Tennessee, by Thomas Nelson. Thomas Nelson is a registered trademark of Thomas Nelson, Inc.

Thomas Nelson, Inc. titles may be purchased in bulk for educational, business, fund-raising, or sales promotional use. For information, please e-mail SpecialMarkets@ThomasNelson.com.

Unless otherwise noted, Scripture quotations are taken from The New King James Version ®. © 1982 by Thomas Nelson, Inc. Used by permission. All rights reserved.

The Scripture quotation marked KJV is from the King James Version of the Holy Bible.

Scripture quotations marked NASB are from New American Standard Bible®. © The Lockman Foundation 1960, 1962, 1963, 1968, 1971, 1972, 1973, 1975, 1977. Used by permission.

Scripture quotations marked NCV are from the New Century Version®. © 2005 by Thomas Nelson, Inc. Used by permission. All rights reserved.

Scripture quotations marked NIV are from the Holy Bible, New International Version®, NIV®. © 1973, 1978, 1984 by Biblica, Inc.™ Used by permission of Zondervan. All rights reserved worldwide. www.zondervan.com.

Quotes by Jim Rohn, America's Foremost Business Philosopher, reprinted with permission from Jim Rohn International © 2010.

Library of Congress Cataloging-in-Publication Data

Flynt, Mike.
  The power-based life : 12 proven strategies to develop strength in your body, mind, and spirit / Mike Flynt.
    p. cm.
  ISBN 978-1-4016-0434-9 (trade paper)
  1. Christian life. 2. Success—Religious aspects—Christianity. I. Title.
  BV4598.3.F62 2010
  248.4—dc22

                              2010017114

Printed in the United States of America

10 11 12 13 14 RRD 6 5 4 3 2 1

To Eileen, Delaine, Micah, and Lily,
my true "power bases"

Contents

Acknowledgments   xi

1. Power Base: Play to Your Strengths   1
2. Basics: Master the Essentials   17
3. Mindscape: Cultivate a Winning Attitude   31
4. Visualization: See What Can Be   47
5. Belief: Defy the Skeptics   63
6. Commitment: Move Forward Relentlessly   81
7. Team: Know Who You Play For   99
8. Identification: Fly Your Flag   117
9. Adversity: Turn Your Difficulties to Your Advantage   133
10. Compassion: Practice Radical Mercy   151
11. Time: Maximize Your Moments   167
12. Body: Sow in Health, Reap a Longer Life   185

Notes   201
About the Author   205

Acknowledgments

Eileen, my pretty lady, you are the best friend I have ever had. You express your love for me in so many ways, and you always make me feel that I'm someone special. You are my "forever love," who saved me from myself, and you overwhelm me each day with your affection and devotion.

Delanie, my lionheart, you have always inspired me to be a better father just so I could come closer to being the perfect man you believe me to be. You are beautiful, smart, and talented in so many ways, but you will forever be that little girl who always placed her total trust in me. You are an amazing, devoted mother with a heart that is never too full to embrace those whom God places in your life.

Micah, my hero, you are a wonderful son, a man of character and integrity who loves the Lord and has amazed me since you were a little boy with your wise decisions about life. My faithful training partner, you always inspired me to be my best physically and walked hand in hand with me as we studied God's Word, increasing our knowledge of him. The years we boxed—our laughter at each other and the many prayers we shared together—are precious memories to me. You are a wonderful father and husband, and you will always be my hero.

Lily, my sunshine, you are a special blessing in all our lives, born out of prayer and in God's perfect timing. You are beautiful, intelligent, and gifted in so many ways. Is it any wonder that you are always so excited about life? I'm blessed beyond measure by so many memories of our make-believe parties and all the father-daughter dances, and by the opportunity to watch you blossom through the years into the beautiful young woman you are today. As with your sister and brother before you, I am so proud of you and I love how I see myself in your eyes; they tell me I'm loved and there's nothing I can't do.

1

....

POWER BASE:
PLAY TO YOUR STRENGTHS

Let me ask you a question: What do you want to be when you grow up?

We all have hopes and dreams, but what we most often dream about is the career that is absolutely perfect for who we are, how we're made, and what we want to become. We sense that if we could only get that one opportunity, we would live a power-based life. I'm referring not to political power or financial power but to the personal power that comes from achieving something significant in life and that allows us to go to bed each evening with the knowledge that the day has been another effective investment of our time.

When I first entered the job world, I was working construction by day and washing dishes by night—right after being kicked out of college. It wasn't where I'd expected to be, but you know how that goes. As kids we want to be anything and everything when we grow up: astronauts or pro athletes or president of the United States. But when the time actually comes to go seek our fortunes, we go to the back of the line and take what we can get. I started at the back of the line. Maybe you did too.

In my first book I told the story of my greatest regret in life—losing my college scholarship and education before I could play my senior year of football for the Sul Ross Lobos. A lot of my dreams seemed to have shattered. I was angry at myself and the world. I moved to Austin, Texas, where a friend and I rented a room at a boardinghouse on the campus of the University of Texas, and I took those two jobs. At least, by washing dishes in the sorority house, I could get my evening meals free. As I ate them, I wondered what future lay in store for me.

I knew my life had nowhere to go but up. There was a lot of anger festering inside of me that I was going to have to deal with. I couldn't walk into a room without scoping it out for potential fistfights and visualizing how I would win each one. I played out thousands of physical confrontations in my mind—and won every single one of them. I'm not exaggerating at all when I tell you that. I'll go into much greater detail in the following chapters because it was this phase of my life that illustrated a startling truth and highlighted a key power base in my life. And power bases are what we're here to talk about.

I might have punched my way into real trouble if I hadn't met my wonderful wife. That was a key change of direction for me as I became focused on starting and supporting a family. I took a step up in the job world by selling life insurance for a short time. But there was also my wife's career to consider; she had been a straight-A student and an English major in college. Her goal was to find a job that played to her strengths yet compensated her as fairly as possible. Eileen decided that court reporting would be a wise target job, which meant we had to move to Arlington, Texas, for her to study that trade. When we settled there, I got a night-shift job building cabinets at a manufacturing plant.

Those were good times for me. My dad had passed along some carpentry skills, and it was really nice working with my hands and putting his teaching to good use. The pay was better than average too. I cared for our daughter by day, my wife did so by night, and we knew we were building a foundation for a solid family life.

Still, I lacked that feeling of doing the essential thing in life I was made to do. Someone has said that the two greatest days of our lives are the day we're born and the day we realize what we were born for. I hadn't quite gotten to that second one yet.

Then again, you know how it is when you're starting a family. I was so caught up with my beautiful wife and my little daughter, Delanie, that I didn't lose much sleep over having the perfect job. My destiny was a work in progress. I wondered what I was going to end up doing and whether it was going to make me happy.

DREAM JOB

As a boy I really hated one thing about myself: my size. I wanted to be big and tough, the kind of guy I knew my dad expected me to be. I've written about how he was a warrior who taught me to be one—how he bought us two pairs of boxing gloves, and how we put on those gloves and went after each other without restraint.

It's true that one of the results of this was that I developed a big chip on my shoulder, but I'm not proud of that. When my dad berated me for getting kicked out of school after yet another fight, I told him that I was exactly what he had made me—and he couldn't argue. He had only wanted me to be able to take care of myself in any situation, but he had created a Frankenstein.

Still, it wasn't all bad. As a result of his challenge, I took my strength and fitness seriously. I had an unquenchable drive to live up to my dad's high standards of masculinity. We have a chapter on adversity in this book, and the message is that what you do with your adversity becomes a power base for you. Since my size was the only thing holding me back, what I lacked in physical stature, I made up for in power. It helped me in football. It was good for my self-image. I felt good and enjoyed having the extra strength. And of course, optimal physical conditioning is good for you too; it becomes its own reward.

That's why I maintained my body condition even when football appeared to be over for me after my junior season in college. There was no way I was going to let my muscle tone or percentage of body fat slide after working so hard for so many years to maintain them. Wherever we lived, I found health clubs and training facilities, and I cared for my body the way some guys cared for their expensive new sports cars. Training was a daily discipline, like brushing my teeth or taking a shower. And it was something I truly enjoyed. I loved the whole goal-driven world of conditioning, and the "good kind of tired" I had after an intense workout.

I was lifting weights in a gym one day when I struck up a conversation with a guy who had a job that caught my attention. He told me he was a strength coach at the college level.

His name was Boyd Epley. He worked at the University of Nebraska, where he had once been a track star, but was in Arlington, Texas, for the National Power Lifting Competition. We hit it off and talked in detail about our shared love of weight training, and he saw that I was a former college player with a powerful drive for excellence and a love of the weight room. Three days later he offered me a job as a graduate assistant strength coach at Nebraska.

What a break! Is it possible to achieve your dream without having realized in advance that it was your dream? I've become persuaded that many of our dreams are pursuits we haven't even figured out. It is only God who knows what we would ask for if we were smart enough to realize it in the first place. Listen to how the Bible backs me up on this:

> But we are hoping for something we do not have yet, and we are waiting for it patiently. Also, the Spirit helps us with our weakness. We do not know how to pray as we should. But the Spirit himself speaks to God for us, even begs God for us with deep feelings that words cannot explain. God can see what is in people's hearts. (Romans 8:25–27 NCV)

That was me, hoping for what I didn't have yet. And isn't it nice that God sees what is in our hearts and moves us toward those things that are for our best, when we can't even figure out what they are?

If I'd known there was such a thing as strength coaching, I would have been all over it! This was actually a brand-new profession at the time. I hadn't realized there was a growing science of weight training; I'd just picked up a few pointers in gyms here and there. I immediately embraced the idea of working with young men and women to help them be the best athletes they could be.

POWER-BASED LIVING

The point of all this is to demonstrate how there was a perfect profession for me, just as there is for you. Strength coaching was just the right fit. It enabled me to work in an environment I loved, and it allowed me to teach and encourage younger people—something I found truly fulfilling. This job was active, physical, goal oriented, and connected to sports. For me, what was not to love? I had found the career path I was born to follow.

I've since followed it in new directions with my invention and promotion of the Powerbase Fitness system, a logical career development for me. Our goal throughout life should be to keep fine-tuning our work to match the way God has wired us, to the extent that we understand who we are at that point in time. During the journey, we grow, and our environment changes. The road takes new turns for us, and we find new and more advanced ways of fulfilling our destiny—just the way God drew it up for us in his game plan.

Okay, enough about me. Let me ask you again: What do you want to be when you grow up—and why?

This is a book about power-based living—it shows you how to use power-based principles to help you realize your life's goals and dreams. There are identifiable points of power in this world and in our common experiences, and if we can find and maximize those, wonderful and fulfilling adventures will characterize our lives.

A quick glance at the table of contents will identify which power-based principles we're going to explore. The only thing they have in common, other than being key issues of life, work, and interpersonal relationships, is that they are supported by biblical truth. I personally try to navigate my life from a biblical Christian perspective, but let me also point out that these power points work for *everyone*. They work simply because they are true and because they reflect the conditions of this world as we commonly experience it.

You'll notice that I share verses from the Word of God in every chapter, and I speak from the viewpoint of a follower of Jesus Christ. Even if you haven't made that choice in your own life, I hope that the practical good sense of these directives will ring true with you.

When I worked with student athletes at the collegiate level, I noticed that many of them loved playing video games. Some of them played computerized football, and some of them fought in virtual wars or to combat aliens. In these battle-related games there are little areas or items known as *power-ups*. When players move their onscreen characters across these items, they suddenly gain extra power, extra health, or extra ammunition. The strategy is to move through these graphic landscapes and look for power-ups.

So it is with the principles in this book. They are power-ups for your journey toward finding true significance and effectiveness in life. As you read, I hope you'll constantly be reminded that every single one of these ideas has a direct application for your life. I'm convinced that if you can learn to seize upon each of these power-based principles, your life will be much more effective and satisfying.

YOUR STRONG PLACES

Now back to this idea of playing to your strengths. What strengths are we talking about? I like the idea of the "sweet spot," that place on any tennis racquet or baseball bat that will drive the ball just where you want it to go. A great tennis or baseball player will learn to work from the sweet spot. But we have them too. We're made to do certain things particularly well. You know you've found that spot when you find yourself thinking, *I'm really in my element when I do this.* For you, it could be working with people. It could be handling details, or it might be something more creative.

In the next few paragraphs, I'm going to tell you more about the process of finding out just where your abilities lie. But I'm guessing you already have a pretty good idea about it. You've figured out that you have areas of strength and other areas that, well, someone else should be handling.

I found my sweet spot when I discovered it was possible to have a career in strength training. I learned how much more fulfilling life could be when I played to my strengths. It's our first power-based principle—the foundational concept for the whole series of principles because it's the one about who you really are and what you choose to do with your life. There's an incredible power that comes from finding what we were designed to do in life. And yes, I believe that most of us have one tailor-made direction that constitutes our very best chance for making an impact in this world. That doesn't mean there aren't people who could be successful in multiple career paths. You and I have both met people like that. Any number of life goals would probably make you happy. But each one of us is uniquely and delicately crafted to do specific things.

For example, I did fine in construction work though it didn't thrill me. I was pretty good at cabinetmaking and derived a certain satisfaction from making a high-quality piece of furniture with my hands. Perhaps I could have had a nice career in that field. But I knew all the time that there was something out there that was the thing I was placed on this earth to do.

Meanwhile, how was I spending my spare time? When I wasn't with my wife and daughter, I was working out at the gym. I wasn't dragging myself in there—I looked forward to it! I talked with other guys about how to better maximize a workout. Some athletes hated the "drudgery" of strength training, and they abandoned it the moment their playing days were over. Not me. And when I met a guy like me whose career was in that field, my eyes lit up. "What?" I asked. "You mean people *pay* you to do that?"

That's the first principle of playing to your strengths. Think about what you would do for free, do joyfully, every day of your life. And ask yourself a crucial question: Does it provide a true service of some kind? I might like taking a Sunday nap, but no one will pay me to do that. However, I did find something I loved to do that offered value to someone else.

People go to career counselors and take extensive tests that assess their aptitudes. These are very helpful inventories. But the best way to find out what you were meant to do is to ask yourself two questions: What makes my eyes light up? What do I do that helps people and would still do if no one paid me? Find the very best answer to these questions and then play to that strength.

By the way, don't assume that this self-questioning is a given, and that it's something people are already doing. In his book *Now, Discover Your Strengths*, Marcus Buckingham reported on a Gallup poll that surveyed 1.7 million employees from 101 companies in 63 countries. These workers were asked what they did and what they were *good* at doing. Only 20 percent of them stated that they were using their strengths every day. That means that in the workplace, four of every five employees are being misused, set up for personal frustration.[1]

It's no good for the organization, it's no good for the employees, and it could be the reason why we see so many people that are unhappy with their jobs today.

Organizations shift employees around based on the moment's need rather than the individual abilities of each person, never considering what the long-term consequences could be. And when someone does well with a certain responsibility, he is sometimes promoted to a job that pays better and has more status, but that may no longer represent his strengths. Is that corner office with the window worth the price of less effectiveness and less personal satisfaction?

We are often just as guilty of seeking work based on the pay rather than the job profile. It's nice to have a slightly higher salary, but we should also consider whether we're truly matching our unique abilities to the task. God made us for specific purposes, not specific pay scales. He also made us to live joyfully and passionately. The right task has much more to do with joyfully fulfilling our purpose than the compensation it brings us.

Let's examine another misconception about talent and ability.

ACCENTUATE THE POSITIVE

Management expert Peter Drucker has written, "To build on a person's strengths, that is, to enable him to do what he can do, will make him effective . . . to try to build on his weaknesses will be frustrating and stultifying."[2]

Yet very often we give an excess of attention to the areas in which we struggle. Birds aren't very good at walking, but you don't see them spending their time trying to improve their skill. What they do is fly. Horses feel no anxiety over their inability to fly or to climb trees; they are designed to run and experience no qualms over the things they weren't designed to do. Why, then, do we probe ourselves for weaknesses and beat ourselves up over them?

Jim Kaat was a baseball pitcher though in recent years you might recognize him as a broadcaster. As an active player he could throw a mean fastball. He said that his success began in 1966, when he worked with ace pitching coach Johnny Sain. Sain would quietly watch each of his pitchers perform; then he would call them in for private meetings. He asked Kaat about his four best pitches. "My best is my fastball," Kaat answered with confidence. "Then comes my curve; then my slider and changeup are third and fourth."

Sain nodded and asked, "Which do you practice the most?"

"Slider and changeup, of course," said Kaat. "If I master those, I know I'll have a big season."

Sain said, "Well, I've got a different idea. Work on your fastball. That's the one you love to throw. During practice, warm-ups, and during the games, make that your focus and see if you can make it an even better pitch. See what happens if you throw it 80 to 90 percent of the time you're on the mound."[3]

This was the last advice Kaat had expected. Wasn't the pitching coach there to fix what was broken? Anybody could do what he could already do! Jim Kaat wanted to be the master of a whole arsenal of pitches. But he did what his coached asked. That season Kaat threw a steady diet of fastballs, his best pitch. He won a staggering twenty-six games in the American League and was named the best pitcher in the league, second in the majors only to Sandy Koufax of the Los Angeles Dodgers.

Think of it as refusing to throw good effort after low potential. Instead, feed the highest potential in yourself. And if that seems too obvious, think about the ways we work together in groups. We cross-train people for flexibility, rather than power-train them for specialization. We play musical chairs with departments and responsibilities as if people were interchangeable rather than singular, unique creations made by God with distinctive strengths and just as distinctive weaknesses. I'm not saying it isn't good to be versatile, but it's better to be a master of one skill than mediocre at several.

The Bible tells us, "For we are His workmanship, created in Christ Jesus for good works, which God prepared beforehand that we should walk in them" (Ephesians 2:10). That means that not only has God prepared us to do our work—but he has our assignments laid out and waiting for us to "walk in them." As a mother comes into her child's room in the morning, lays out the child's clothing for the day, and gently wakes that little boy or girl, God has our task set out for us and is eager for us to find it and begin hitting on all cylinders.

None of us can spend all our time in the roles that are most comfortable for us. But we can certainly be aware of our areas of strength and be intentional about maximizing our opportunities to use them. In other words, each one of us needs to find his or her fastball and throw it as often as possible.

FINDING YOUR STRONG AREAS

How well do you know your tendencies, your personal strengths, and your blind spots? How much of a "people person" are you? Do you tend to see the forest or the trees more clearly? Personality testing can be helpful in giving you a handle on how you're put together. Those who work in the human resources field often have access to inventories that can reveal just what our tendencies are. The most basic of these may be the popular DISC inventory, which divides people into four very basic styles of relating to others.

If you're assertive and aggressive, tending to step up and lead individually, you might be a D (dominance).

If you tend to rally people together and lead by consensus, you could be an I (influence).

You would be an S (steadiness or submission) if you are patient and supportive, loving consistency and preferring to be helpful by staying in the background.

And you'd be a C (conscientious) if you are a highly disciplined person and tend to work alone.

Everyone has one of these styles or, more accurately, some combination. There are many other, far more complex personality inventories as well. These tests aren't perfect. These are better measures of how we see ourselves than of how we really are. But they often do a very good job of showing just what we do best and where we struggle. For example, if you come to understand yourself as a high C on the DISC inventory, you can learn to accept that you're terrific at going off to your corner and working out a solution to a complex problem. What you don't tend to do well is stand up in front of people and make a persuasive speech. No one can possess every virtue; your strengths are always going to be accompanied by balancing weaknesses. Therefore, you should celebrate the thing you do well and stop worrying about the way God *didn't* make you.

Even better than tests, life itself is the best inventory for learning about how we are made. It's amazing how much we learn about ourselves the moment we hit the real world of work. A young lady might have seen herself for years as a schoolteacher, but then she spends a year in classrooms and discovers it is the last thing she should be doing. How many are sent off to medical school or law school by ambitious parents only to come to the conclusion that they really want to work with the homeless or be musicians?

The painful fact is that the ambitions we work out, or our parents work out for us, don't always match the way we're wired. And we simply won't find a sense of joy and fulfillment until we're plugged into the right socket.

I talked to my friend Rob about this concept and discovered how his career journey has taught him about himself and helped him find what his dream *should* have been. Growing up, he thought he wanted to be a cartoonist. He was pretty good, maybe even good enough to make a living at it. In any case, getting a job after college meant going into the family business, a manufacturing firm where he worked in customer service for several frustrating years. What he learned was that he had no real interest in the product being manufactured, no aptitude for the science of the products, and too little patience with the customers who called to badger him about their orders. During this period, he began to see himself as a person with tremendous character flaws. Nothing is worse for the self-concept than unproductive work.

Finally, Rob decided to trust God, resign, and seek some new direction. He took an interim job directing a ministry in his church. The experiment was a great success. Rob was certain he had found his calling because this time the product was something he was passionate about: following Christ. For a few years things worked out. This was a time when he started feeling a little better about himself.

But the job brought out what he continued to see as his character flaws. For instance, he was tremendously disorganized, which made it difficult for him to organize ministry tasks. There were times when he would still become frustrated and impatient with people. However, over a period of time he watched how he did his work and discovered that he was gravitating toward certain tasks within his job description. He loved writing Bible study curricula for the teachers and group leaders, some of which were successfully published. And he spent a great deal of time on the ministry newsletter. More times than not, he found himself wishing he could simply stay in his office and work on the responsibilities that involved writing.

Eventually, Rob moved on from church ministry and became a full-time writer. He realized he had always enjoyed writing and been good at it but had never considered it as a viable career direction. People had told him that the field was too competitive, but the truth is, if God has made you to do something, there *will* be a way to do it. Sometimes the best advice of our loved ones isn't based on the best insight as to our skills.

Rob found himself working mostly on books about Christianity, the subject he was passionate about. All the qualities he didn't have, the flaws exposed in his first job, were irrelevant to working on books. "I wouldn't consider any other career, no matter what it was," Rob says today. "I love the written Word of God, and I love writing on the subject of faith. What I can't believe is that someone will pay me to do it!"

Now, that's what I'm talking about. Did you notice how each career change got him a step or two closer, philosophically speaking, to where he needed to be? Did you also notice how he learned important clues about his personality mix along the way? What he discovered is that we not only feel terrific when we do what we love, but we also love ourselves in a more healthy way when we do it. We realize that it's invalid to judge ourselves based on our flaws rather than our strengths. If you're no good with a fastball, maybe the slider is your thing.

Or maybe you should take up golf.

PLAY TO YOUR SPIRITUAL STRENGTH

Another example of the importance of playing to your strengths is found in the spiritual world. As in the business world, we tend to ignore this principle entirely in the spiritual world. However, the Bible teaches that we each have unique spiritual gifts, which are not the same thing as talents. They are generally connected to personality types and abilities, but they are direct spiritual applications for serving the church.

Peter wrote, "Each of you has received a gift to use to serve others. Be good servants of God's various gifts of grace. Anyone who speaks should speak words from God. Anyone who serves should serve with the strength God gives so that in everything God will be praised through Jesus Christ" (1 Peter 4:10–11 NCV). And in Romans 12:6–8 Paul listed seven key gifts: prophecy, service, teaching, exhortation, giving, administration, and compassion.

The idea is that each of us has a spiritual gift or a certain mix of them. And the church only functions as it should when people know and use their spiritual gifts. You'll find that the average believer has no idea what his or her gift may be even though those gifts are sitting and waiting to be discovered and used. Again, we assign tasks in church based on other issues. "How about being a teacher for our youth?" we say, without thinking about whether or not this man or woman has a teaching gift.

So often churches can be dysfunctional because they're not playing to the strengths of the people who attend. As a matter of fact, pastors are expected to have every strength imaginable. We expect our preachers to be stained-glass superheroes. If you look at the list of gifts in Romans 12, you'll agree that a pastor is expected to do nearly all these things. He must be a great teacher, of course, as well as specifically having the gift of exhortation, which means the ability to convince people to practice what he preaches. He needs to have the gift of compassion, or his people will find him cold and uncaring. He is expected to have some gift of administration and to be highly organized even though many of the best teachers are dreamers rather than detail people.

I wish everyone who attends a worship service could understand that our ministers aren't born with extra gifts, nor are they *reborn* with extra spiritual gifts. They are people like us, and we set them up to fail when we pound on them for the things that aren't part of their gift mix. The church was never meant to be a one-man show with a few hundred spectators. The idea is for all of us to be empowered by putting our gifts to work. We are all ministers. If you attend church, let me suggest that you take the lead in seeing that the shepherd and sheep alike begin playing to their strengths. When that happens, your congregation will begin bearing fruit as never before, and everyone will experience fulfillment rather than frustration. You'll also see God's people begin to resemble the church described in Acts 2.

How do you find your spiritual gift? A number of organizations publish spiritual gift inventories, and some can even be taken online for free. Find out what God meant for you to do within his body of believers.

BUT I'M NOT GOOD AT ANYTHING!

We all know people who on the subject of spiritual gifts will say, "I don't have one." And on the more general subject of strengths will say, "I don't do anything particularly well. I'm just kind of an average individual." Phillips Brooks said, "It is almost as presumptuous to think you can do nothing as to think you can do everything."[4]

No one is a human void, lacking a character profile and gift mix. Everyone can do certain things well even if they are not flashy things. If you were to study some of the most successful business leaders in our society today, what you would find is that many of them are people who would never strike you as particularly gifted. Let me give you a good example.

For many years television commercials for Wendy's restaurants featured the man who built that franchise, Dave Thomas. Thomas, who passed away several years ago, was extraordinarily ordinary. He had a problematic childhood; he was adopted, and his adoptive father kept remarrying and moving to different cities. Dave Thomas was no brilliant student in school and dropped out in the tenth grade to work full-time.

Taking an entry-level job at Kentucky Fried Chicken, Thomas worked hard enough to move up from busboy to manager. Col. Harlan Sanders himself was Thomas's mentor and taught him some of the secrets of managing a fast-food franchise.

Earning the opportunity to manage all of KFC, Thomas was a millionaire by the time he was thirty-five. He reversed the direction of a failing business and in 1969 left the company to found Wendy's. Over time, what he discovered about himself was that he was a hard worker who wasn't very detail oriented. He was good at inspiring those around him; he was a natural-born cheerleader. He also understood the marketing side of things. But it was best for him to surround himself with people who were much better with day-to-day tasks. In this way, he was free to travel throughout the country to visit various Wendy's locations and encourage their managers.

Wendy's grew quickly through the seventies and eighties because Thomas understood what was good for the organization. He did not need to be too hands-on; he simply needed to understand his limitations and devote himself to what he did best. If you remember any of his television commercials, you know just how he came across—just an average guy, someone who didn't look out of place by the milk shake machine, as folksy as your uncle.

It's amazing how many great leaders would never strike us as anybody particularly special in terms of gifts. They may not be tremendously charismatic individuals, riveting speakers, or have brilliant academic credentials, but they understand what they do particularly well and know what skills they need to rely on others to supply. They play to their strengths. It's their key to enhancing their effectiveness.

During the 1800s D. L. Moody was the Dave Thomas of Christianity. He built an empire of Christian ministry—churches, publishing houses, colleges, seminaries, mission groups, and other organizations and institutions. Moody left a legacy that still serves God throughout the world even though he was a shoe salesman, a very average public speaker, and had no great shakes as a theological thinker. The only extraordinary thing about him was his compassion for the emerging problems of people living in cities. When God called him away from selling shoes and on to helping people know and love God, he began to surround himself with gifted people who could do the things he couldn't do. Listen to what he said on this matter of ability: "If this world is going to be reached, I am convinced that it must be done by men and women of average talent. After all, there are comparatively few people in this world who have great talents."[5]

UNLOCK YOUR STRENGTHS TODAY

In the days when stagecoaches carried people and all of their worldly possessions across the prairies, the wagons were often waylaid by various kinds of robbers. Sometimes it was the Apaches who would wait in ambush, surround the stagecoach, and seize whatever interesting possessions they found inside.

One day a group of Apache warriors made off with a safe filled with gold. It was heavy, and it took several horses working in tandem to drag it away to their village, but eventually they got it there. They had learned about guns and many other curiosities from the visitors from the East. They were eager to witness the amazing things inside this iron box. They tried exposing the safe to fire, but it didn't affect it. They pounded on it with rocks for hours, but their efforts made no difference. They turned the knob around and around for hours, but it didn't open the door like other doorknobs they had seen.

Finally, the Indians dragged the safe up a hill and cast it off the cliff, but when it hit bottom, the door remained shut. With great disgust they abandoned the safe and all the gold inside it.

When the Apaches were gone, the original owners of the safe, who had watched from a distance, came to reclaim their property. Because they had the combination, all the gold inside was available to them.

That's the way it is with the strengths inside you. You are the lockbox, and your abilities are your gold. Sometimes we become very frustrated as we try to make our way in this world. We sense that the treasure is there for the taking, but we can't get to it. All the dreams in the world and all the talents within us are wasted when we don't have the right combination to help us break through and put them to work.

Playing to your strengths is the first of the gold coins in the lockbox of your personal potential. Think of each of the principles that follow as further resources, greater opportunities to be the very best you can be in God's plan for your life. Let's get started!

2

Basics: Master the Essentials

Most people would agree that, over the last few years, I've taken the road less traveled. I have to say that nobody has been more surprised by my life than me, the guy who has lived it.

I never expected to become a college football player at the age of fifty-nine. Nor did I anticipate becoming the inventor and entrepreneur who would create the Powerbase Fitness exercise system and watch it spread through school systems, military bases, and families across America. I've served as a strength and conditioning coach at Nebraska, Oregon, and Texas A&M. I've married a wonderful woman, raised children, and held my own grandchildren.

I had done a lot of things, but I came to realize that I was being driven by one thing I hadn't done.

In high school I played for Odessa Permian, the football team immortalized by the book and film *Friday Night Lights*, and was on its first state championship team. The University of Houston, during its glory years, offered me a full football scholarship, but I ended up at a much smaller NAIA college.

While at Sul Ross I was a team captain and by my junior year the leading tackler on the team. I had only one problem: I majored in getting into fistfights. And as previously stated, the school kicked me out before I could play my senior season. That hurt deep down inside me, and I didn't realize for a long time that I hadn't quite gotten over the disappointment of missing my senior year of college football. Depriving myself of that senior year, wondering what might have been, was the greatest regret of my life. It gnawed away at my psyche until, finally, during a story-swapping session at a reunion of Sul Ross players, one of my former teammates challenged me to do something about it. If that was my greatest regret in life and I felt I could take the physical punishment that was surely to come, then I needed to quit complaining and check out the possibilities. To my amazement, I had a year of eligibility left, and I was going to play it out at Sul Ross State University.

My wife understood though it took some fast talking on my part. She supported me in my efforts to follow through with this wild notion. We sold our house in Franklin, Tennessee, and moved to Texas. The rest, as they say, is history—you can read about it in my book *The Senior*. I can tell you that when I played out that lost season, I didn't run into any other grandfathers blocking, tackling, or throwing passes. I had two kids who were older than my teammates, and I was eight years older than my head coach.

I didn't uproot my life and relentlessly pursue this goal in order to become a cute newspaper story or a locker room freak show. I didn't want the players to take it easy on me, and I didn't want anyone's sympathy the first time I got knocked on my butt. Due to my lifelong commitment to fitness and my Powerbase training system, I was able to compete in the weight room with those kids, who were a third of my age. It was obvious that they were impressed by my physical abilities, regardless of age, and they told me how much they respected me for what I was doing. I loved my teammates, but I knew I would before I ever met them. I just love kids.

The game had changed quite a bit between 1970 and 2007, the gap between my junior and senior seasons. Football, like everything else, grows and evolves. But the game hadn't changed nearly as much as I had. As a younger athlete I never had the benefit of seeing the "big picture" that is visible from the vantage point of my age. When you are twenty-one years old, you think you are bulletproof, and everything seems possible. By the time you're approaching threescore years, you know your limits. You can see the glories and the agonies of life in much better perspective.

I brought some of that to the locker room. The jarring contrast of being a walking anachronism, an older man in a young man's game, brought out a host of new insights about life, about navigating the different ages and stages, and about compromising with people instead of getting into constant fist-fights with them as I once did.

I had also gone from being a rebellious kid to becoming a man who loves and encourages kids. I've spent a great deal of my adulthood trying to do all that I could to point younger people toward better lives. There was a time when the kids around me were either my teammates, with whom I was knocking heads to compete for playing time, or the players on the other team, with whom I was knocking heads to knock them down.

I worked for years as a strength-and-conditioning coach, helping young men and women optimize their bodies physically and, of course, build their characters in the process. It was strange, after all those years, to return to the head-knocking part with a new perspective on the guy at the next locker or across the line of scrimmage.

AS TIME GOES BY

In my younger days I was all about being a self-made man. That was my point of pride. It was me against the world, and I could and would accomplish any goal I wanted, simply by bullishly doing it on my own. In a way, it's an American thing, being the Marlboro Man, the self-reliant, rugged individual who takes life on his own terms and sets his own course. My favorite song at that time in my life was "My Way" by Frank Sinatra. It seemed I was always biting off more than I could chew.

But there was one eye-opener that was by far the greatest of all. I returned to the world of football as a follower of Jesus Christ. Sports had been my old passion, but now I had a passion for Christ that reordered all my priorities and showed me my old world through new eyes. It's kind of strange: I was advanced in age, but I had a younger man's body and a child's faith, which Jesus says we need. I was all over the map, wasn't I?

In the past, nothing had been more important to me than being tough. Now it was important for me to be loving. While my former life had been built on a foundation of self-reliance, I knew now that I needed other people. And though I had lived constantly on the cusp of violence with a chip on my shoulder, now I was motivated by bearing others' burdens on my shoulders.

I could see that I had changed far more than the game to which I was returning. Football had a few new offensive and defensive strategies. The wishbone was out and the spread was in. But it was still basically a game about moving an odd-shaped leather spheroid across a one-hundred-yard field. It still involved eleven men lining up to move forward and eleven to stop them. My own life, however, was a whole new ball game.

One thing was true of both of us—football and Flynt. I realized that whether we're talking about punting or people, it all boils down to the fundamentals.

Time has taught me that another line from an old song is true: "The fundamental things apply as time goes by." It does not matter what you're setting out to accomplish. It could be losing thirty pounds, painting a house, or studying to becoming an authority on Southeast Asian history. Whatever you're trying to do, there are basic truths you must discover and master.

Getting the basics right makes all the difference. The least capable person who does that will be more successful than the most gifted individual who doesn't. That's why I was able to do certain exercises, in spite of being a few months shy of sixty years old, that some eighteen-year-olds, approaching the prime of life, could not do. That's why some of the greatest coaches in each sport tend to have been the least physically gifted in their youth—since they couldn't coast on what God gave them personally, they had to master the fundamentals that God set up for everyone. Because they did so, they became the ones most capable of coaching others.

John Wooden was one of the most successful college basketball coaches in NCAA history. His UCLA teams made regular trips to the national championship game. One year, on the first day of practice, the new hotshot recruits couldn't wait to see what gems of masterful coaching he would impart. They were beyond high school now, and they couldn't wait to take their games to a new level. But Wooden went down on one knee and began showing the players how to put on a sock.

Put on a sock? Had the old man gone around the bend?

As Coach showed the proper way to neatly but firmly slip the sock over the toes, he explained that he'd seen too many players pull on their socks in a haphazard way, thereby creating wrinkles. Once the full-court game got going and the players were turning on a dime and sprinting back up court and down court, those wrinkles began to create blisters. And players with blisters invariably saw their game go down a couple of notches.

Therefore, that day's lesson was how to properly put on a sock.

Wooden didn't win ten national championships in twelve years by doing things the way everyone else did. He accentuated the basics, the fundamentals, whether it meant perfecting the jump shot or dressing the foot. Sometimes the fundamentals are so simple you don't even think about them.

Don't get me wrong—we're not just talking about athletic issues. There are fundamentals for tax accountants. There are fundamentals for house-keeping and growing a garden. You don't want to leave your car with a mechanic who doesn't follow the basics of engine care. What if a surgeon were about to operate on your heart? Wouldn't you want to know that he was well-schooled and current in the basics of heart medicine?

Whatever the subject, whatever the task, it all boils down to fundamen-tals. During my coaching years, standing on the sidelines of football games, I can't tell you how many times I watched a player drop a critical pass or let a punt ricochet off his hands and become a fumble because he was thinking about which direction to run rather than "looking in" the ball and being sure he caught it. That's the bottom-line fundamental of receiving passes or returning kicks. If you mess up the primary thing, you don't get the chance to do the secondary thing.

That's what I want to discuss in this book. As I look around our country today, I see a lot of desire in people to accomplish things. But I also see people unable to reach first base due to a lack of effort. It's all about the fundamentals.

A PERFECT PRACTICE

Most of us from the sports world have shared an enduring fascination with the late Coach Vince Lombardi, who built the Green Bay Packers from an NFL doormat to a championship dynasty. He would begin each summer camp in much the same way John Wooden did. He would hold the pigskin high and say, "Gentlemen, this is a football."[1]

This was Lombardi's way of saying, "Get off your pedestal and get ready to work. You don't know as much as you think you do. We're going to deconstruct your whole idea of how to play this game, go back to the very foundation—the ball, the one essential thing needed for a game—and build excellence from there."

So relentlessly did Lombardi drill his players on the fundamentals that they became relentless practitioners of perfect execution, play after play. He forced his players to get it exactly right—not partially right or nearly right.

And he did this through sheer repetition. Lombardi once said, "Practice does not make perfect—perfect practice makes perfect."[2] His offensive linemen worked themselves beyond exhaustion to achieve the perfect block, then to be able to duplicate it over and over. Defensive players had to tackle with absolute precision so that the other guy never broke a tackle. Fumbling wasn't tolerated among running backs. The players hated him with a passion all the way through training camp—then by the end of the season, they all but worshipped him. He had made them better than they ever believed they could be. He had taken a scattered roster of people with varying abilities and molded it into one unified team of flawless performers.

But it all started with the fundamentals, then the rough, sometimes dull business of practicing the fundamentals. Perfect practice makes perfect. Lombardi's players often spoke of running the same plays over and over in practice every day until they could basically make every move in their sleep.

It could not have been any more fun for the head coach and his assistants than it was for the players. There is nothing thrilling about repetition, and this is often the problem we find with people who fall short today. We can handle a diet or an exercise program or a Bible-reading routine for a week, but we can't do it for a month then another month. We want excitement. We want to be entertained. But the thrill of receiving the Super Bowl trophy is all about the drudgery of practicing in the dirt and dust on many sweltering August afternoons.

Lombardi finished his career with the Washington Redskins. One hot summer afternoon in late July 1969, someone from the front office knocked on the coach's door at just about the time to go out on the field and informed

Lombardi that *Apollo 11* had just landed on the moon. The Redskins' office was recommending that practice be postponed for half an hour so the players could see the historic moon walk, something that had never occurred in the history of mankind.

"Won't do it," said Lombardi. "It won't help those astronauts to have us sitting around watching them, and them walking around up on the moon won't help to make us better football players."[3]

Practice went on as usual, right on time. He did call the team into a circle and told them what was going on. He gave a little pep talk about courage and then asked the players to join him in a prayer for the nation's bold astronauts. Then there was a hard, fiery practice.

How much of the secret of success in life—in any venture—can be captured right there, so simply? Fundamentals plus practice. Find out the most basic things you're supposed to do; then do them over and over and over until you do them perfectly. Author Jim Rohn has said, "Success is neither magical nor mysterious. Success is the natural consequence of consistently applying basic fundamentals."[4]

What does that mean for you? Perhaps you have a reason for picking up this book. It could be that you need a little inspiration for chasing after your dreams. You have your own invention you'd like to see in use all across the world, or you'd like to begin a business of your own. Maybe there's some goal that seems unreachable to you. If you and I were sitting here in my office having a personal conversation, just the two of us, I would first ask you, "What is it you're setting out to do?"

Second, I would ask you, "What have you learned from your mentors about how to do it?" In other words, if you want to open a restaurant, how many entrepreneurs have you studied who have been successful in doing so? What were the fundamentals, the basics that they revealed in being successful? And finally, how can you begin to practice doing the things that will finally make it happen for you?

I believe that if you could give a clear answer to each of those questions, you could then create a game plan for achieving your goal. That's how obscure individuals make their mark on the world. That's why the winner of the biggest game in the world, the Super Bowl, receives a trophy named after an obscure former lineman for Fordham University, as well as a semipro player for the Brooklyn Eagles: Vince Lombardi, the NFL's greatest coach.

THE WHOLE CYCLE

Through my own years as a player, then a trainer of players, I came to understand that lesson about the importance of basics. Kids would come in at eighteen, gifted but not too mentally tough, maybe a little pudgy. By the time they were seniors, if they responded to our program, they were well-drilled on the basics, not only of a game but also of a disciplined way of life—of caring for their bodies, fighting toward their goals, and becoming winners off the field as well as on it.

I worked with both men and women and came to see that some really understood the importance of fundamentals, regardless of their gifts. One of the most amazing female athletes, by the way, was Babe Didrikson Zaharias, one of the true pioneers of track and field, who showed just what women were capable of doing athletically during a time when there was little encouragement for them to make the effort. She won five first-places in track and field at the 1932 Olympic tryouts. Then at the games themselves she finished with medals in the high jump, 80-meter hurdles, and javelin throw—all requiring different skills. They say she could run, jump, or ride. She could play basketball and baseball equally well. Quite obviously she was born with physical gifts other men and women can only dream about.

But those skills were God-given gifts. What impresses me most about her was that she didn't cruise through life on those God-given abilities. No, in 1935 she took up golf! That sport had little to do with the speed and power that were her natural attributes. Many men and women spend their lives focusing on their golf game. But Zaharias took it up after being the best in the world at far more physically challenging athletic endeavors.

She found the best coach available and studied golf intensely—she studied the basics though it meant starting at the bottom. When she first entered the PGA tournament, she missed the cutoff score to remain in competition, but she did meet her husband there. And through the next two decades, she became America's first female golf celebrity. "Except perhaps for Arnold Palmer, no golfer has ever been more beloved by the gallery," wrote a reporter in the *New York Times*.[5]

I tell this story to make a point that people so need to hear these days. It's far less about your gifts and talents than you may think. If you have the right amount of humility (what I call "coachability") and determination, you can be successful in nearly anything. You'll find that those who score in life are often people who might have scored in many other directions than the one they chose. It's not necessarily what God gave them but what they did with what they had. Winners simply choose their path, begin working on the fundamentals, and practice until they approach perfection as closely as humanly possible.

I learned this lesson about sports and achievement some years ago. Yet as a young Christian, I knew very little about the basics of my faith. It simply didn't occur to me that the spiritual world had its own solid basics. I knew about worshipping God. I understood about living by the golden rule, obeying the Ten Commandments, and following the advice of the Sermon on the Mount. What made the difference for me was digging into the Scriptures themselves, far deeper than those obvious passages. I learned about the scope of biblical prophecy and God's guidance of history and how every word of the Bible is genuinely inspired.

Well, that caught my attention. I had not realized the treasure I held in my hand when I picked up a Bible. The words inside took on new weight for me as I began a spiritual workout regimen of reading it and applying it every day. For the first time, the daily walk of faith made sense to me. The words I was reading were no less than the basics, the fundamentals of the spiritual life.

Having discovered that, how could I be anything but a disciplined student of the Scriptures? I know all too well that a football player who never enters the weight room, who lies by the pool during the summer, is never going to see the playing field during the fall. In the same way I am astounded by the number of Christians who believe they can be serious about their faith without ever being serious about the Bible. You can no more read it once in a great while than an athlete can tend to his or her physique once in a great while. Is it just me, or is that just plain old common sense?

In my years as a strength coach, my weight rooms always had a certain progression of machines. Some worked the muscle groups of the arms and chest, some various parts of the lower body. A disciplined athlete is going to move through the whole cycle though he will give special attention to the lifts that are the most helpful at the time. A quarterback might be working to strengthen his throwing motion, and obviously a kicker wants to develop those muscles that will enable him to produce a booming kickoff. But kickers work on their upper-body strength, quarterbacks work their legs, and players are going to take advantage of every apparatus in the weight room to mold the strongest, healthiest, most durable body possible. Why not take advantage of the opportunity?

That's why we have all the parts of the Bible. People tell me, "I spend all my time in the Gospels," or "I stick to Paul's letters and a few of the psalms." Well, it's okay to have areas that are your favorites, but I wonder how many people realize that the Bible has very specific sections and is carefully organized to help us *go through the cycle* and get the full workout?

I'm going to walk you through the whole arrangement, just as I'd help a newcomer to the Powerbase Fitness system or a football player in the weight room. The Bible is intimidating to so many people simply because it is large and unfamiliar to them. Those are false fears. If you were raised on some island apart from civilization and then saw a modern weight-training room, you wouldn't know what to think, would you? You would suspect you were looking at a high-tech torture chamber. (I have known some who would say you weren't far wrong.) But every machine would be there for a specific purpose to improve your health and overall wellness.

You don't need to be intimidated by the Bible. You just need to know what is there, how it works, and why it helps you. Then you will want to move through the cycle regularly.

Ready for your demonstration?

THE GRAND TOUR

The first few books of the Bible are all about history. Why do we need to know the history of the ancient Israelites? Because it helps us understand, as nothing but a good, exciting story can, who *we* are and who God is. Ageless wisdom is always contained in history. Why did I have more wisdom when I returned to football at an advanced age? Because I had a history. Why do young people do such foolish things? Because they have no history. Time is the greatest teacher there is.

The Bible's history books tell us everything we need to know about our own universal weaknesses as people. We learn what practices made Israel (and its leaders) spiritually strong and what influences led to destruction. We notice cycles of nearness to God and drifting from him. I see myself in these histories, and this section of the Bible gives us countless stories of men and women and how they related to God.

Then there is a section of *wisdom* writings in the Bible. There is no history here but songs (Psalms); wise sayings (Proverbs); an intriguing book of simple, practical, and shrewd philosophy (Ecclesiastes); a book about romantic love (Song of Solomon); and an epic about why bad things happen to good people (Job). If the Bible were a brain, this section would be the seat of the emotions. If you haven't spent time in the books of wisdom, you've missed an essential part of your workout. The Psalms in particular express nearly every human emotion, from joy to mourning to anger, in the forms of prayer and music. They are beautiful and inspiring, and just when you find it hardest to connect with God, you discover a psalm that says exactly what your heart feels.

The last section of the Old Testament is equally fascinating: the prophets. The amazing and often strange men in this section came along as history moved toward the coming of Jesus Christ. The nation of Israel had fallen apart, and these *megaphones from heaven* spoke out to remind people of their lost spiritual heritage. Very often they spoke of the coming Messiah or deliverer: Jesus. A verse in Micah, written hundreds of years before Christ was born, accurately predicted that he would be born in Bethlehem. A number of passages in Isaiah described Jesus' ministry and even that of John the Baptist, the *advance man* for Jesus. Long before the events, the prophets described nearly everything Christ did, and they also offered a few clues about the end times yet to come.

Don't feel bad about being bewildered by the Old Testament. We have so many great resources to shed light on any passage we might be studying. Buy a good study Bible from your local bookstore—one with plenty of margin comments, graphs, maps, and timelines—and you will find yourself fascinated by the scope of the Old Testament books. And you will learn things about God you could never learn otherwise. Reading and studying all parts of the Old Testament is one of the fundamentals, and you wll never achieve your spiritual goals without attending to the basics with a disciplined approach.

The New Testament is just a bit simpler. For one thing, all of its books were written closer together in time, perhaps within a fifty- to sixty-year span. The first four books, of course, are parallel accounts of the life of Jesus. Each one has a slightly different intention, based on its target audience—whether Greek or Jew, for example—so together they give us a well-rounded picture of the greatest life ever lived. The book of Acts is a sequel to Luke's gospel. It opens with Jesus' ascension to heaven and follows the progress of the brand-new church. It introduces a great man named Paul, who wrote many of the letters that follow. Disciples such as Peter and John wrote other short letters, giving us our most direct instructions on how to live the Christian life. Again, the letters, written to churches of the era, all have different emphases. Finally, the book of Revelation is the bookend of the Bible, showing the end of time just as Genesis shows the beginning. We follow John the apostle as he gets a glimpse of the coming new world—God's perfect city—that will follow when time comes to a close.

USING THIS BOOK

The Bible is truly a foundational fundamental of the faith—try saying *that* several times quickly.

The book you're presently holding, on the other hand, is *about* the fundamentals. That's a big difference. I hope that as you read it, you will keep your Bible nearby so you can explore the verses quoted here. I want my book to be helpful to the readers who pick it up, but the Bible, God's Word, should be read by every follower of Jesus Christ (as well as everyone else so that they, too, might find the joy of becoming followers of Jesus Christ).

We are going to explore what I believe to be the basics needed to live a power-based life, but all of them will be founded on what we already know from the Scriptures, which is God's complete revelation of the things you and I need to embrace in order to enjoy success in this life. That book has laid out the fundamentals of living. It tells us how the game is played on a daily basis and what exercises and regimens we need to follow if we want to become all that God has in mind for us.

For example, we've talked about the basics in this chapter, right? Listen to how the Bible lays the foundation for this point. In Revelation, Jesus is speaking to one of the ancient churches that has done a good job in the past but isn't quite hitting on all cylinders. He speaks to that church, commends it for working hard, for holding out high standards, and for getting through tough times. But he points out one problem among that group of people: they've lost their "first love." You know the way you felt when you first met your life mate? How about when you first became a believer?

That's the excitement of first love, and we're supposed to hang on to that. Sometimes, of course, we go into the doldrums. So Jesus, in this passage, gives the antidote. Listen to what he says: "Remember the height from which you have fallen! Repent and do the things you did at first" (Revelation 2:5 NIV).

In other words, take a moment and remember how you used to feel about things. Consider the difference between then and now, "the height from which you have fallen." Then repent: that means turn completely in the other direction and just walk away from the things you are doing now that you know are wrong. And "do the things you did at first." Do you recognize the theme of fundamentals? Those are the things we do first and the things we tend to drift away from. Maybe we need to learn how to put on our socks again. Maybe we need to realize just what it was that attracted us in the first place to the very aspect of life that needs work right now. Maybe we need to start all over with the fundamentals.

It encourages me to know that I'm not the first guy to struggle. That church in the Bible had run out of gas and needed some good advice—yet it had helped lay the foundation for the greatest faith in world history. As a matter of fact, every single hero and heroine of the Bible, from Adam to Moses to David, and from Peter to Paul, made great mistakes (in many cases, major-league sins) at one time or another. If the Bible were a book of myths and legends, it wouldn't tell their stories so candidly. The characters would be like Hercules or Superman: bigger than life and impossible to identify with.

But we can all relate to Moses, who said he stammered and could not speak to Pharaoh as God wanted; to David, who struggled with lust; and to impetuous Peter and overbearing Paul. I love the fact that the Bible doesn't make me feel small and weak but gives me hope that, if God did not abandon a sinner on the scale of King David (murder, lying, and adultery in one fell swoop!), then perhaps he can use me too.

If I can see myself through the characters of the Bible, then I can look to Jesus—the only one who never failed, the only one who never committed a single sin, the most courageous, loving human being of all history—and I can see the pattern that God, through his Holy Spirit living within me, wants me to conform more closely to every single day.

That's what happens each morning when I make the choice to spend time on the fundamentals of my faith through reading Scripture. I see myself in the good but imperfect people who walk through all the pages of my Bible, and I know my soul so much better. Being honest about who I am, I can then focus on who I can become through Christ. For decades of my life now, this has been the most powerful period of every single day. For me to start each day without God's Word would be like stepping onto the football field without my helmet. There is no way I can play the game of life and ever hope to succeed without this fundamental staple each day.

So to paraphrase Lombardi: This, gentlemen and ladies, is a Bible. Inside these covers is where we go for practice every day, and even if people walk on the moon, nothing is going to postpone that time each day in the Word of God. Then, from there, we are going to extrapolate several fundamentals for life, always using the words of Scripture to demonstrate the point, to help you understand that it doesn't take a wise philosopher to see the Bible's application to our lives.

Let's begin with an absolute essential: attitude.

3

Mindscape:
Cultivate a Winning Attitude

For thirty-six years I carried around the burdensome baggage that was my greatest and deepest regret—I had been kicked off the Sul Ross football team for reasons explained in the previous chapter.

Pursuing my dream was a big decision for me. Have you ever wanted to do something but didn't have the confidence to try it? Have you ever tried something that no one else has ever done before? What about stepping forward to do something that might cause you to be laughed at—not only by the people around the table who are aware of the challenge but also by a whole world of strangers? Those were some of the questions that confronted me.

Many of us reveal our deepest dreams while talking to a spouse or a best friend only to receive a similar challenge. Say you've always wanted to open a restaurant. "Well, why don't you?" asks your spouse. "Go for it!" says your friend. "Just do it," urge the folks at the water cooler.

And how do you reply? "Oh, I could never do that!" And you begin the litany of reasons for not trying. You're pretty creative at that moment, taking the trouble to think of new reasons. Wait a minute! Why are you going to so much trouble to stop your dreams in their tracks?

WALKING THE PLANK

It takes a measure of courage to believe in oneself. An attitude driven by fear, rather than confidence and faith, keeps us lurking in the shadows of our comfort zones, wondering what life would be like out on the open horizon where people make breakthroughs and achieve exciting new things.

I heard a story about a great football coach whose team was being beaten by a couple of touchdowns at halftime. In the locker room the players were sitting on their benches with their heads down, already beaten in their own minds. The coach scanned the faces and knew there wasn't a chance at winning—not unless the players started believing in themselves. He suddenly barked out an order so abruptly that many of them flinched. "Get up on your feet!" commanded the coach. "Get in a line and go walk across that bench, the one at the far end, left side to right."

The players looked at him as if he were out of his mind. Were they being told to walk the plank, pirate-style? Where was the x-and-o strategy for the second half? They just shook their heads and obeyed, each player stepping up on the ten-foot bench, easily walking across it, then hopping down from the other end.

"Now," said the coach. "Anybody fall off?" The players chuckled nervously. "Nope," he continued. "Each one of you easily walked from one end to the next without even thinking about it. Was anyone afraid?" Lots of eyes rolled.

The coach said, "Okay then. How about if I take this same board, nine inches wide by ten feet long, and suspend it between two skyscraper windows on the thirtieth floor and have you walk from one building to the other? How many of you would volunteer?" Lots of eyes stared.

"Just what I thought," said the coach. "Same board, same feet, same guys. Just a second ago you would have hopped across on one leg and done so easily. But change the setting, and not one of you would do it though it's physically just as easy a task. The difference is *risk*. You won't do what you're capable of doing because you're preoccupied with fear. Right now, you're playing this game as if you're on a ledge thirty stories high. *The difference is not physical—* it's between your ears. Now go out there and do what God has given you a body capable of doing. Play physical, fundamental football and win."

They did just that.

The problem in that situation was not on the outside but on the inside. We say that on any given day, any team can beat any other team, and one of the primary reasons for this is clearly the attitude of the players. There are coaches and programs who simply know how to win, and they nurture a winning attitude. They believe in themselves, and it creates an infectious atmosphere of confidence and expectation. Just a few individuals with powerful, positive attitudes can affect an entire group. It's true of teams, of businesses, of churches, and of families.

IT'S ALL IN THE ATTITUDE

I'm reminded of the story of a little boy outdoors alone, playing baseball with his ball and bat. None of his friends are home, so he has to create the game in his mind. "Okay," he narrates, giving the play-by-play. "The greatest hitter in the game steps up to the plate. He comes in with nine straight homers!"

He tosses the ball about ten feet high, straight upward. As it comes down, he makes a mighty swing, worthy of Mickey Mantle. *Whooosh!* He misses. The ball plops onto the turf at his feet.

He picks up the ball and says, "Strike one! It was a nasty curveball, but the All-Star hitter is ready to *cream* the second pitch!" And with that, he tosses the ball skyward again and lets forth with another swing, an uppercut that would clear the bases . . . if there were bases. *Whooosh!* But again, the ball nestles into the grass between his feet.

The little boy picks up the ball and scowls at it. He says, "Strike two! A brand-new pitch, one never invented. But the Hall of Famer means business now. He leans in, glares at the pitcher, and . . ." Up goes the ball and around goes the bat. It's a masterpiece of a swing, one that would surely send the ball out of the neighborhood, beyond the school district, and maybe into the adjoining county. Babe Ruth himself never had such a swing.

Yet for the third time, he has connected with nothing but air.

The boy looks at the ball for a second, stoops, and picks it up. A wide grin comes to his face as he drops the bat and says, "Okay! The *greatest pitcher in the game* has just struck out another one! That's nine straight strikeouts!"

I love that story, a version of which I heard in a song by Kenny Rogers. It's a brilliant word picture of a powerful and infectious attitude. The boy made the choice to find something positive in his failure.

Your attitude is the single most important aspect of who you are and the leading indicator of where you're going. That may sound like a broad statement—I certainly thought so the first time I heard Chuck Swindoll proclaim it in a sermon. But life has taught me that it's true. As I watched young football players come through the programs where I worked, it became clear that there were kids with world-class talent who weren't going to enjoy freshman class success. There were others who came in with very modest ability yet were bound to excel. As a matter of fact, I knew for certain they were going to achieve the highest results in the classroom and everywhere else. The difference was attitude.

Men and women with positive mental attitudes don't have to find the one job they can tolerate; they'll master any job they take up. They'll make the workplace better for everyone else. And what others consider drudgery, they'll transform into an adventure.

By the same token there are men and women who travel through relationships and marriages, discarding each one like an ill-fitting sweater. They just can't seem to make a go of anything. A few years ago I heard about a celebrity who was getting his sixth divorce. While discussing him, a young lady sighed and said, "He just can't seem to find the right mate." I would beg to differ—sometimes it seems increasingly likely that the rest of the world isn't the problem.

CIRCUMSTANCES ARE HIGHLY OVERRATED

But what if the circumstances are impossible? You might say to me, "Mike, my situation is a little different. I work for an impossible boss, and I can't find another job—not in this economy. I am discouraged, and nothing I can do is going to change the way my boss acts." You might have a damaged marriage or there might be a health problem. Sometimes there are crises and challenges that are bigger than we are—or at least they seem to be. Let's just say that there are times in life when we are powerless to change the circumstances.

Let me ask you to consider something: Is it possible that we are focusing on the circumstances, which we know we cannot control, rather than on the one thing we can?

Anyone can throw a pity party and curse the unfairness of the world. It requires no skill, talent, or vision to do that. By the same token there's another thing that every single one of us can do—we can determine our attitude. Now, I'm not talking about letting a smile be your umbrella or having a Pollyanna mind-set that is all about retreating into some personal fantasy world and pretending that cold rain is a warm beam of sunshine. This is not mental dishonesty we are describing. No, I'm talking about a power we can unleash, which will transform us from the inside out and can very often have an effect even on seemingly hopeless circumstances.

Viktor Frankl wrote a book called *Man's Search for Meaning*. Even though it is largely a book of philosophy, it sold ten million copies and was named by the *New York Times* as one of the ten most influential books in the United States. Frankl was a prisoner in a Nazi concentration camp during World War II. Like all of those arrested by the Germans, he was stripped of all his possessions and separated from his family. His wife and his parents were executed in other prison camps. Frankl's very identity, he wrote, was taken from him.

As a prisoner he agreed to use his medical skills and to serve as a doctor. He set up a suicide watch unit and spent all his time surrounded by desolate, despairing souls. What he concluded from his experience and wrote in his book was that every single moment of life has meaning, even when that life is drenched in suffering.

> We who lived in concentration camps can remember the men who walked through the huts comforting others, giving away their last piece of bread. They may have been few in number, but they offer sufficient proof that everything can be taken from a man but one thing: the last of the human freedoms—to choose one's attitude in any given set of circumstances, to choose one's own way.[1]

When we can't change a situation, he reflected, we are challenged to change ourselves. On one occasion he spoke to a great number of prisoners who were being starved because they were protecting a fellow inmate. Everyone was miserable, and Frankl said that on any occasion of testing and trial, it helps to imagine someone looking down upon us—a parent, a spouse, or God—who believes in us and expects us to persevere.

Reflecting upon his years of torment, Frankl came to the conclusion that the hundreds of prisoners he had observed were all free agents even though they were not physically free. They faced suffering, but their peace, well-being, and chance of survival were determined by the attitudes they chose to adopt, rather than the circumstances they could not control.

Our enemies may receive the power to fully determine what is around us, but they can never touch what is inside us *without our permission*. It is the one freedom that can't be taken away. And remember that Frankl didn't compose this philosophy from the comfort of an easy chair next to a warm hearth. He came to believe it after the Nazis took and killed his wife, did the same to his parents, impounded all his possessions, and let him starve and freeze in the worst of conditions.

We hear of a story like that and realize that a difficult boss—or the day's aggravation, whatever its nature—may not, in fact, be the greatest obstacle any human being has ever faced. You need only open your Bible to the New Testament to notice that a great many of its books were written by people suffering through terrible persecution. Frankl faced a bleak concentration camp, but Paul faced beheading; Peter faced the same crucifixion that Jesus endured. Yet what is the theme of all these books? Joy! Triumph! Inner peace! I think those writers have something to teach us about attitude. Let's look a little deeper.

GLAD-ITUDE

The apostle Paul was a former rising star among the Jewish religious scholars. He had a comfortable lifestyle, Greek education, and Roman citizenship. In many ways he had it all. When he encountered the risen Jesus on the road one day to a town where he planned on arresting Christians, he was changed from the inside out. He spent the rest of his life traveling across the known world, sharing Jesus with everyone he could. He faced stoning, starving, illness, imprisonment, and ridicule. Some of his letters were written from prison, yet they crackle with joy. In the book of Philippians, for example, he spoke of his desire to know Christ better:

> Not that I have already obtained all this, or have already been made perfect, but I press on to take hold of that for which Christ Jesus took hold of me. Brothers, I do not consider myself yet to have taken hold of it. But one thing I do: Forgetting what is behind and straining toward what is ahead, I press on toward the goal to win the prize for which God has called me heavenward in Christ Jesus. (Philippians 3:12–14 NIV)

What attitudes come across to you as you read that chapter? Humility. Eagerness. Vision. Joy. This from an energetic traveler forced to cool his heels under house arrest. This from a man who had an expansive agenda but no opportunity to carry it out. This from a man who might have been saying, "God, I've sacrificed a great deal to do your work. Is this how you take care of me?"

Instead, Paul wrote as if he had the world on a string. Following Christ is an adventure that can't be taken away, not by Romans or Nazis or anyone else. It's an attitude summarized by Paul this way: "To live is Christ and to die is gain" (Philippians 1:21). That is, heads I win, tails I also win! Staying on earth means the joy of serving Christ, even from a prison cell; death just means an eternal reward so wonderful we can't even imagine it now.

You might call that *glad-itude*. It's a mind-set of thanksgiving to God that is like a flame the world can never extinguish, no matter how much water it pours on it.

Think now about your own life. Is there anything about it that would keep you from thinking like the people I've offered as examples in the last few paragraphs? Is there any reason you can't cultivate a positive mindscape and grow it into something beautiful?

You might ask, "What is a mindscape?" Just as you can look outside your window and see a landscape, inside your head there is a mindscape. It's demonstrated by the way you speak, the way you react to challenges, and the energy by which you pursue your dreams. James Allen wrote a classic book called *As a Man Thinketh*. The title comes from the Bible verse that reads, "For as he thinketh in his heart, so is he" (Proverbs 23:7 KJV). Allen wrote, "A man's mind may be likened to a garden, which may be intelligently cultivated or allowed to run wild; but whether cultivated or neglected, it must and will bring forth."[2]

In other words, you're going to grow roses or weeds inside. It's your mindscape, so the choice is up to you. If you want crabgrass of the cerebellum, that's your business.

We have a tendency to focus on the negative things going on in our lives, and it's that harsh focus that many times creates the problem. Our emotions, for one thing, get in the way. Disappointment can cloud rational thinking so that a lot of negative self-talk runs through the brain: *Nothing good ever happens to me. God must not love me very much. Life is so unfair, and I'll never get a break.*

When we stop to consider each of those statements, we know they don't hold water. But they stay inside us and have power over us anyway until they become self-fulfilling prophecies. For as we think in our hearts, so are we.

You might call this type of thinking *bad-itude*. But just remember, we are not talking about bad *people*; we are talking about bad thought systems—and we will talk more about that toward the end of this chapter. Just know that no failure is final. It is important for us to remember that this is a bump on your personal road, not your identity. The road leads onward far past that bump; it's going to lead to wonderful destinations, and you must simply follow it.

WHAT DEFINES US?

During my senior season of 2007, our Sul Ross team had a tough game against an in-conference rival. Hardin-Simmons University had a proud athletic tradition, winning from eight to ten games per year over recent seasons and regularly going to the NCAA tournament for our division.

Hardin-Simmons clearly had more resources than we had at our program, and it was clear from the outcome of their games that they had more talent too. Naturally, we had a deep desire to make our mark as a team by prevailing over Hardin-Simmons. You can just imagine how I felt, playing a single season of football in a thirty-seven-year period—every game was an opportunity I had waited decades for and would never have again.

Hardin-Simmons was ahead by ten points late in the fourth quarter. However, we had fought hard to seize the momentum and were now driving down the field to score and narrow that gap. The clock, ticking away far too rapidly, dictated that we needed to get a quick touchdown, attempt a successful onside kick, get into field goal position, and send the game into overtime.

That's a tall order, of course, but there was absolutely no margin for error. Even if we executed every play perfectly, there was barely enough time for the two scores we needed to survive. Along our sideline the air was charged with emotion and adrenaline. Every player was fixed on the common goal that united us.

One of our wide receivers was a gifted young man named Sean Collins. He had been turning in a star performance on the field throughout the afternoon, making acrobatic catches, saving drives, and getting us in position to score points. Now, in the huddle, his number was called one more time. When the play began, our quarterback threw a long pass across the middle to Sean. Once again, he made a terrific and very difficult catch, and the best part was that he kept his feet. Sean broke a tackle and turned toward the end zone. The players, our coaches, and our fans caught our collective breath.

Sean broke a tackle, but it set him off-stride. Before he could build up speed, a cornerback slammed into him. Sean again twisted free. He was just a step from getting into the open when a safety hit him from behind. He kept his feet one more time, but the tackler slapped the ball loose. Hardin-Simmons pounced on the ball, got possession, and then ran out the clock to give us a bitter defeat.

Afterward, in the locker room, Sean was emotionally devastated. Of course, nobody blamed him. His teammates offered nothing but comfort and encouragement—we win as a team, we lose as a team, as any properly coached player knows.

I told Sean that he had given a supreme effort, not just in the desperation of that one play but throughout the game. There had not been a snap of the ball when he had not laid it all out and sacrificed his body for the benefit of the team. Without his contribution, I pointed out, we would never have gotten into position to challenge for the win against a team like Hardin-Simmons.

As a matter of fact, if we'd had twenty-two guys like Sean, we would have won that game by a large margin. He needed to do nothing but hold his head up.

Here's my point: Sean was not defined by the fumble. His identity was seen far more accurately in his intense, uncompromising desire to go up and take the ball out of the air, to keep his feet, to take the physical punishment that comes to receivers who go across the middle, and to do everything in his power to accomplish the goal of his team. *That's* who Sean was—not the outcome of the play.

As a losing team we sat in the locker room ten minutes after time had expired. A loss seemed to be the only relevant issue in the entire universe. It was bitter, it hurt badly, and our minds were filled with "if onlys." If only we had completed one more pass, if only we had forced one more turnover.

But time passes, and it happens quickly. One loss on a Texas football field, even more so, one particular play in that game, will fade into the haze, but the effort Sean put forth was going to go with him into life, into business, into family and faith. If he put that same effort into things other than football, the world would be a radically better place for his involvement in it. And how important is a single fumble back in the day compared to that? The loss hurt for the moment, but I knew Sean was too much of a winner to dwell on one tough play.

Do you see the shift in perspective? That day we got out of the sad locker room and looked at the big picture. We changed our perspective, the essential key to attitude.

LESSONS FROM A DEAD TREE

Imagine you live at the edge of a beautiful, green forest. You sit on your back porch and enjoy the sounds of the birds singing, catch sight of an occasional deer silently grazing, and have a nice path for quiet nature walks.

But one day your favorite tree, an oak, is hit by lightning. After a few weeks it becomes clear that its leaves are no longer growing, and the bark is becoming dry and pale. You call a friend who is a tree surgeon, and he says there is nothing to be done for the ailing tree. It will have to die or be cut down, ultimately to be replaced by a younger one.

So now, when you pour a cup of coffee and sit out on the porch, your eyes inevitably move to the dying oak tree. You miss the way it used to look, and you don't realize you are failing to enjoy the rest of the view. Friends visit and wonder why you don't seem as relaxed when you sit on your porch; they don't notice the graying oak, but for you it dominates the landscape. Without realizing it, you are forfeiting all the pleasure and relaxation you once possessed simply because you can't see the forest for one hurt tree.

That's the way it is when we dwell on the negative things in our environment. Think of a time when some life crisis, minor or major, had you down—anything from a big dent in your new car to an argument with a close friend. Maybe there was trouble on the job front, or you just had a really rough day. Your thoughts probably closed tightly around that one troublesome subject, and if anyone had asked you to count your blessings, you would have given that person a nasty look.

But doesn't that rather trite cliché—*Count your blessings*—contain an undeniable element of truth? You may not want to think about it right now, but the big picture says you've got a lot going for you. Let's imagine something new. As you're sitting there, wrapped up in your troubles, the phone rings. It's a friend who has just suffered a *serious* crisis: an ominous report from the doctor; a spouse who moved out. Isn't it amazing how, all of a sudden, that dented car seems more trivial than tragic?

What has happened is a rapid perspective shift. Your mind's lens had zoomed in on a very small, worrisome detail, and the phone call forces it to zoom out and show the whole landscape. It was just one stricken tree, after all—look how *many* beautiful green trees span the horizon. And listen, there *are* birds singing (even though you couldn't hear them five minutes ago). It turns out you're actually a very fortunate person!

Most people know this, but they overlook it. You and I need to be reminded frequently that *attitude is a matter of perspective.* Just as there are plenty of healthy trees in the forest, there is always—*always*—an infinite list of items for which we can thank God, all of them overpowering the few cares and worries that preoccupy us.

Let me tell you something else about that old tree: it will become fertilizer. Nature renews itself. Everything organic—all that is given life by God—becomes fertilizer for his new creations. It is actually quite comforting to know that the beloved old oak will break up into elements that help younger trees emerge from the fertile soil.

This principle is true not only in the world of biology but also in the world of the spirit. Every dead tree in the forest of your life provides food for the new things God is growing. In other words, failure is fertilizer.

Paul explained it for us in Romans 8:28: "And we know that all things work together for good to those who love God, to those who are the called according to His purpose." That is the Bible's way of saying that God doesn't waste anything, whether it's a dead plant or a failed plan. Every single unfortunate event in your life will serve some positive purpose in God's great plan. That does not mean he is going to tell you exactly how he uses a dented fender or a failed relationship or a period of unemployment. We simply accept that God is awesome enough to use everything for our good.

That can be hard to see when we are hurting. How can God use a terrible tragedy for something good? Think about this. If you were to walk through a shipyard, you would see lots of iron and steel, everything from great beams to tiny bolts. If you were to pick up any piece of iron you found, no matter how large or small, you could be certain that when you tossed it into the ocean it would sink to the bottom. Iron simply doesn't float.

But somehow, through the mastery of his craft, a shipbuilder can take all of those pieces—thousands of tons—and assemble them in such a way that the ship floats beautifully! I bet you've never stopped to think about the miracle of that, have you? In the same way, we look at some unhappy event in life and believe it is impossible that it could be part of anything good. But if a shipbuilder can make that boat float, don't you believe God can take all the bits and pieces of our heavy burdens and put them together into a beautiful plan?

It's called perspective. Take your eyes off the tree and look at the forest.

Then think about the way the remains of that tree will form something good in God's plan, and you'll be on your way to having an entirely different attitude.

ACCENTUATE THE POSITIVE

There's another thing you can do to create a powerful, positive mindscape:

> Finally, brethren, whatever is true, whatever is honorable, whatever is right, whatever is pure, whatever is lovely, whatever is of good repute, if there is any excellence and if anything worthy of praise, dwell on these things. (Philippians 4:8 NASB)

Did you catch the key word? *Dwell.* What does that mean? The dictionary will tell you it means to go somewhere and stay. We've been talking about dwelling on failure, which is one of the most self-destructive ways to manage the mind. Paul is telling us to dwell on things that are good, lovely, excellent, and praiseworthy. As the old song puts it, "Accentuate the positive, eliminate the negative, and don't mess with Mr. In-Between."[3]

Find the good stuff. Go there, Paul said, and *set up camp.* Surround your senses with things that are true, honorable, right, pure, lovely, and of good repute (that means a reputation of solid gold). Let me ask you to stop at this point and consider the environment of your life. Instead of mindscape, now we're talking about *lifescape.* What television shows play in your home? What kinds of books and magazines do you read? It's also worth thinking about the people whom you allow to surround you. Are they encouragers? Do they make you a better person? Or are they sarcastic and cynical?

This is a world filled with negative, cynical influences, and strong people can be weakened by bad influences. The Bible tells the story of Solomon, a king who, other than Christ, was the wisest man who ever lived. In the beginning he was devoted to God and his kingdom was blessed. But in his later years he began to take in many wives and concubines. That was a custom of his day, but the worst part was that he allowed many of these women to bring in false religions. In the end it damaged his rule and split his nation in two. There were other kings of Israel who might have been great, but they surrounded themselves with poor advisors.

YOUR MENTAL GRID

A mental grid is the way we're wired to think. Who puts that wiring in? Very often they are our parents, our influential teachers and friends, and anyone early in life who has a strong impact on us. More often than we realize, we act not on the basis of objective, rational thought but on the basis of the way we've been *programmed* early in life. There is a conscious part of the mind and a subconscious part. With the conscious part you might decide to get up and go look out the window. The subconscious part functions silently, influencing you without your realizing it. It determines how you might feel about certain things you see outside the window. There might be a certain kind of dog that frightened you when you were very little. You have forgotten the incident, but your subconscious mind has not. You react to the dog in a certain way without quite knowing why.

We learn things we don't know we're learning, especially when we're very young. These lessons stay in that subconscious part of the mind. For example, a little boy had a strong perception that his father was very displeased if he didn't like sports or if he didn't play them well. He grew up thinking he had to earn acceptance from other males by being a good athlete, and his entire sense of self-worth was based on that concept. A little girl got the idea from her parents that she would not be loved unless she made perfect grades. All her life she will believe no one loves her unless she constantly works to earn it. That's a bad mental grid that will need to be rewired.

The subconscious mind is a massive hard drive that maintains very detailed files from every experience we have. Very slow to erase themselves, the files influence what we think, feel, and do. The good news is that we can reprogram what is there. If we can learn to control our thoughts, we can control our actions. The Bible tells us that day by day, through the power of the Holy Spirit, we're being transformed to the very image of Christ. It tells us that God wants to give us the mind of Christ.

That's why we must fill our minds with Scripture. The Bible is a power base of dynamic love. If we bathe our minds in it, we'll know that God loves us regardless of all our flaws. He fully forgives every sin. And we can be free of some of the flawed systems of thinking inside our heads. As a matter of fact, the Bible tells us that perfect love casts out fear. It casts out all kinds of bad things. This is why we need to take Paul's advice and fill our lives with things of excellence and true beauty.

It helps to be conscious of the negative thoughts that creep into our lives and stimulate negative actions. We need to catch ourselves in our negative thinking, watching out for thoughts such as, *Nobody loves me unless I perform*, or *God never lets anything good happen to me*. Then we can confront those negative thoughts with the power of what the Bible tells us. Martin Luther, the great church reformer from centuries ago, said that when he felt the devil tempting him or inspiring a bad thought, he visualized sending Jesus to the door to answer the devil's knock. That would always send Lucifer slinking away. What he was really doing was underlining in his mind the power and authority of Christ.

Another good practice is positive self-talk. I'm a big advocate of that. If I verbalize ideas that I know to be true, my conscious mind gets the attention of my subconscious. "Flynt," I might say out loud, "you know better than that. The fact is that God loves you and is filling your life with blessings. Have you stopped to think about how many amazing blessings are in your life today? Or are you just going to focus on that one thing you don't like or don't have? And why don't we confront it in a positive, problem-solving way rather than sulking about it?"

For extra power, quote Scripture out loud. If you haven't memorized any good verses, I've noted some below that are all from that great study of attitude, Paul's letter to the Philippians. Print them on note cards and carry them with you. Try quoting them when you're in need of an attitude adjustment.

- "For it is God who works in you both to will and to do for His good pleasure. Do all things without complaining and disputing." (Philippians 2:13–14)

- "One thing I do, forgetting those things which are behind and reaching forward to those things which are ahead, I press toward the goal for the prize of the upward call of God in Christ Jesus." (Philippians 3:13–14)
- "Rejoice in the Lord always. Again I will say, rejoice! Let your gentleness be known to all men. The Lord is at hand." (Philippians 4:4–5)
- "Be anxious for nothing, but in everything by prayer and supplication, with thanksgiving, let your requests be made known to God; and the peace of God, which surpasses all understanding, will guard your hearts and minds through Christ Jesus." (Philippians 4:6–7)
- "I can do all things through Christ who strengthens me." (Philippians 4:13)

Finally, the Bible tells us to pray without ceasing. What an incredibly positive concept: Open the hotline to heaven and just keep the dialogue going! You don't need to be in your special room to pray. You don't even need to close your eyes. You can pray in your car or at work, while you're making the bed and doing dishes, while you're going to sleep and while you're waking up. Prayer is communion with God, and there is nothing on earth that can do more to rewire your mental grid.

The Bible says, "Be transformed by the renewing of your mind" (Romans 12:2). That's what we're talking about. What steps will you take today to begin building a new and powerful mindscape?

4

....

Visualization: See What Can Be

The year is 1970, and the scene is a little bar in Alpine, Texas. I'm a college football player with plenty of attitude and not much maturity. Add to that scenario the roughnecks, cowboys, and other football players living in West Texas at that time, coupled with alcohol, and you've got any number of occasions to fight.

I'm swigging a beer and shooting the breeze with a few buddies. But at every moment I have one eye on the door to the street. I'm watching for some guy who could walk in at any time.

I don't know the guy's name—call him the next guy and the guy after that—because it's nobody in particular. I'm going to size up every male who walks into that tavern. I'm looking for any potential troublemaker, and when I see one, I'm going to watch a little movie inside my brain starring that guy and me. The script will be the same every time, just remade over and over with a different costar.

In the movie this guy and I are going to come to blows. Then I'm going to win. That's the whole script, but the action is *very* detailed. A lot of it actually happens in slow motion so that I can get every little move exactly the way I want it to be.

Now, the interesting thing about this is that I'm multitasking even though in 1970 that term hadn't come into vogue. I am in the film room of the mind, taking careful notes, but at the very same time I am laughing and swapping jokes with my friends in my corner of the bar. Nobody but me knows that a barroom brawl is going on in my mind, with bottles breaking and chairs splintering.

What counts is that I'm now ready. I realize there's a low probability that I'll end up in a fight with that guy, but if it happens, who do you think is going to win? It's probably the last thing this other guy would ever think about. But me, I've written a detailed game plan.

I know, I know. This is not normal behavior or healthy behavior. A guy who thinks like this needs a certain amount of solid counseling. But this was my life nearly forty years ago.

It came about because my dad wanted me to be prepared. He was from a hard-knocks generation. He had lived through a national depression and been to war. He had waited in a freezing foxhole into which a German could leap or a grenade could fall at any moment. He wanted his son to be mentally ready for anything that might transpire. If I wasn't going to be fighting the Battle of the Bulge, then I should at least be ready to fight the battle in the barroom or wherever else I might be.

And it worked. I won a great number of fights in which, by all rights, I should have taken a beating. In each case I had already been victorious, time after time, on the battlefield of my mind.

On camping and fishing trips, Daddy often laid out the rules for being ready at all times. The detail was amazing; he had really thought things through. For example, he counseled me never to sit on the inside of a booth, where I couldn't get to the floor quickly; I should let someone else sit there. I wasn't supposed to step outside to fight with someone, where the guy might have cronies waiting, but instead I was to take care of business right on the spot. I shouldn't let anybody get close enough to something he could grab and use as a weapon—that kind of thing. Fistfight preparedness was an art and a science.

Well, sometimes we create our own reality based on our thoughts. That is actually what this chapter is about. During a three-year period while I was in college, I was arrested five times and broke my right hand at least six times.

Yes, I ultimately came to my senses. I realized I didn't want to go all the way through my life having fistfight after fistfight. It might even be a good idea to try getting along with people. But it's a funny thing how life works. Daddy loved me a lot, and he did teach me a powerful discipline in that my mind was on *red alert* at all times, but I was misusing it. My blood pressure was constantly heightened, and many fights must have happened simply because I expected them to.

But it *was* a powerful discipline. Once I began putting it to different uses, I really had a grip on something. I would go so far as to call it a power-based principle, and to me it is one of the most exciting ones. Let me tell you what I did with the discipline my dad taught me.

AN INSIDE GAME

As my dad walked through all the possible scenarios that could occur, I became fascinated with the whole idea of mental preparedness. Couldn't I use this concept for more *constructive* applications?

As a football player I gravitated toward the film room, which I saw as an extension of the mental discipline. A lot of my teammates were bored silly by sitting in the dark, watching game films. But I saw an opportunity to grab a real advantage by storing in my mind the mental images of the other team and how they played. In visualization you create the picture of yourself in a future situation. These movies already showed the situation in perfect detail. I could run the film in slow motion, see myself on the field, and play the game several times mentally before it was ever contested in the real world. In one actual game I made twenty-four tackles, and I believe that visualization made the difference.

But isn't this purely a self-help concept? When we discuss this subject of visualization, we need to be very careful. There are many pseudoscientific ideas floating around on this topic, and I don't endorse any of those. A recent mega bestseller, both in book and video form, popularized the supposed Law of Attraction, which holds that we can change reality by visualizing what we want. In other words, if you wanted a better job, just thinking about it long and devotedly enough would ultimately cause someone to call you up and offer you a better job. Scientists call that *magical thinking* in a justifiably derogatory way because there is no reasoning, no true causation behind such wishful thinking. We would all like to believe that we could make the world a different place simply by thinking it into being, but there is only one God, and only he is able to do that.

No, that's not the kind of thing we're talking about. When I speak of visualization, I mean something that is verified by science as well as good old common sense. We don't change the outside world as the Law of Attraction claims. We change *our own minds*. When I envisioned myself in a fistfight with the guy over near the door, nothing I did had any effect on him, his ability, or his performance. I only enhanced what I myself could do by preparing *my* mind and *my* attitude.

Sports psychologists have led the way in popularizing this idea of visualization. There have been various studies in its effectiveness, including one in which Russian scientists compared four groups of Olympic athletes by the way they trained. It went like this.

- Group 1 used 100 percent physical training.
- Group 2 used 75 percent physical training and 25 percent mental training.
- Group 3 used 50 percent physical training and 50 percent mental training.
- Group 4 used 25 percent physical training and 75 percent mental training.

Test Group 4, the one that had the highest percentage of mental training, put up the best performance numbers. "Mental images," the study concluded, "can lead the way to muscular impulses."[1]

Dr. Charles Garfield had worked closely with NASA, studying the mental preparation of astronauts who were placed in a simulated environment and rehearsed every single contingency before going into space. He decided to study people who were successful either in athletics or in business, and he came to the conclusion that nearly every world-class athlete or highly successful businessperson was a visualizer. When these people had their breakthroughs or set their athletic records, they were only doing things they had previously done countless times in their imagination. As Stephen Covey would put it, they began with the end in mind.

In the medical world, it has been shown repeatedly that positive visualization can have a dramatic positive effect on diseases as serious as cancer. The mind has far more power than most of us imagine. Indeed it's the ultimate power base.

Marie Dalloway, who has worked with Olympic and other athletes, agrees that peak performers are invariably people who insist on imagining the details of their success. They may not even have realized it or done it consciously, but they have thought themselves into better, more focused performances by thinking in great detail and repeatedly about how they wanted to do their thing.

Dalloway pointed out that even in an informal practice, Jack Nicklaus would mentally rehearse his shot before he hit the golf ball. Every small detail of the shot would be included in his mental rehearsal: the swing, the club meeting the ball, the trajectory of the shot, the landing, the roll, and the final resting spot of the golf ball. He even ran the imaginary film in reverse! Once the ball had landed, he would slowly make it redo all that it had done but backward. You certainly can't argue with his results.

Bill Russell used the principle in yet another sport: professional basketball. And he was doing this in the early fifties, long before sports psychology emerged and became popular. He was eighteen and would ride the team bus across the countryside from one small town to another, specifically imagining how he was going to defend all kinds of offensive moves in the approaching game. The end result was that he became the game's best shot-blocker. Once the game started, he said, "It seemed natural, almost as if I were stepping into a film and following the signs. I was so elated I thought I'd float right out of the gym."[2]

NOT EXACTLY NEW

The Bible tells us, "For as he thinks in his heart, so is he" (Proverbs 23:7). Notice it doesn't say, "As he thinks in his heart, so is the world." We have no promises that we can change the conditions of reality outside the confines of the personal mind, other than through the power of prayer and the purposeful intervention of God. But as we think in our hearts, so we become.

This idea of positive imagination is at least as old as that ancient proverb. The Greeks wrote about it, and ever since then we find it throughout history. For example, the Duke of Wellington defeated Napoleon at Waterloo. It is said that the duke won the battle before it was ever fought by laying out the map, representing his forces with small figures, and simulating every possible move his enemy could make. He looked down at the board and saw the battlefield as it would look from the clouds. He was doing the same kind of mental preparation that athletes—and yes, modern soldiers—do today.

Nathaniel Hawthorne wrote a famous story called "The Great Stone Face," based on a real-life rock formation in New Hampshire that resembled a great, wise face looking over a valley. Its picture was on the state's quarter and on its automotive license plates, but several years ago it finally crumbled and fell. In Hawthorne's story a young man gazed on the face every day because of a legend that the most noble of persons would someday bear those features.

Various businesspeople and leaders stepped forward to offer their faces as perfect matches. But after many years others pointed out that it was the quiet young man himself who resembled the Great Stone Face. He had reflected on its expression for so long and so intently that he had taken on not only its physical qualities but also the inner nobility he admired in it.[3]

Hawthorne was recognizing the truth of Proverbs 23:7, just as people have done for thousands of years. In fact, the Bible constantly underlines these ideas of godly meditation and the power of our thought: "I will meditate on the glorious splendor of Your majesty, and on Your wondrous works" (Psalm 145:5). Paul wrote, "If there is any virtue and if there is anything praiseworthy—meditate on these things" (Philippians 4:8). Charles Spurgeon, the British preacher, said that prayer and meditation are twin sisters—both entirely necessary to the Christian life.

Visualizing the "glorious splendor of [God's] majesty," of course, is a long way from seeing yourself beat the daylights out of someone in a tavern brawl. But this is the idea: fill your mind with positive images of what you would like to accomplish.

Dawson Trotman, founder of a Christian ministry called the Navigators, believed that the last thought in our minds before going to sleep carried special power, so we should be intentional about making that thought a special one from God's Word. He called this the HWLW principle: His Word the Last Word. How often have you gone to sleep with some distressing issue on your mind and had it enter your dreams and cause you to wake with a frown on your face? Why not give positive ammunition to your subconscious before it takes over on the night shift? David wrote, "I remember you while I'm lying in bed; I think about you through the night" (Psalm 63:6 NCV).

Let's think a little bit more about the subconscious mind.

GATEKEEPER OF THE MIND

As we all know, we have conscious thoughts—the ones we're aware of thinking—and subconscious ones, which are the thoughts going on in the brain's basement. But this is one important basement because it controls the greatest part of our behavior. The subconscious is the command center of the human mind.

In between the conscious and the subconscious, there is a filter called the *reticular activating system* (RAS). It is actually a complex group of nerves at the base of your brain. As you go through your day, you are going to take in far more information than your mind will want to save. Think of all the things that you see, hear, feel, smell, and taste. The RAS indexes all this information and takes advice from you on what is important and what isn't. It is a power base in your brain because it is the gatekeeper for what has prominence in your mind.

Let's say you are out driving your car. As you pass a Ford Mustang among many other automobiles, your RAS will normally say, "Just another car of no importance." You will see the car but not be particularly aware of it. But let's say you have recently made a conscious decision to buy a Ford Mustang next week. Your RAS now indexes this item as something important to your thinking, and you suddenly seem to notice Mustangs everywhere. They have been there all along, of course, but you now have that car indexed differently. The

RAS is identifying what is significant to you based on what you deem to be a priority at the time.

An important fact about the RAS is that it doesn't differentiate between real and imaginary stimuli. So when you rehearse an event that is important to you and you visualize yourself succeeding in it, the RAS never shrugs it off and says, "Yeah, you wish!" It sees what you're imagining the same way it sees the real thing. If you imagine winning an Academy Award, your RAS has no way of differentiating that from a genuine event.

Therefore, you are empowering your subconscious mind when you visualize success. Add in the fact that most experts believe the conscious mind only controls a small percentage of our actions; the subconscious controls anywhere from 83 to 95 percent, depending on various research findings. Most of us have no clue just how much of our behavior is not rational, premeditated, and intentional but motivated by things that lurk in the backs of our minds. That is why visualization can be a critical key to changing the way we think and the way we act.

For example, let's turn this argument on its head and consider the *negative* possibilities of visualization. I'm afraid this form of imagination is much more common in people than the positive form. *Fear* is often another word for negative visualization. In the 1960 movie *Psycho* there is a famous murder scene that occurs in a shower. For months after its initial release, many thousands of viewers of that movie were afraid to take showers. Their conscious minds, of course, knew that no one was coming into the bathroom with a knife. But the negative visualization was so powerful that after seeing the film, they followed irrational actions.

Émile Coué, the French psychologist, once said, "If imagination and willpower are in conflict, then invariably it is the imagination that wins." He was talking about just how powerful our basement thoughts really are even when they conflict with what we consciously want to do.

There are much more subtle forms of fear, of course. We fear rejection by other people, and then we repeatedly imagine it happening and make ourselves just a little more hesitant around others. We fear failure at work, and we rehearse all the awful things that will come to pass if we do fail. The more we dwell on these negative images, the more power we give to our fears. The more we index negative possibilities as central to our lives, the more negative our lives become.

I hope you can see what this issue comes down to: Visualization is not some exotic exercise, like transcendental meditation, that you may or may not elect to practice. Visualization is something we all are doing every single day. We are processing thousands of images every few hours, and these images are shaping our thought processes and outlook. Therefore, we must take control over what ideas and pictures we allow to be fed into that amazing computer that is the human brain. Garbage in, garbage out—we all have heard that one, and it's true. But treasure in, treasure out is just as true.

What can you do to start visualizing a better future today?

STEPS TOWARD SEEING WHAT CAN BE

As you can tell, the concept of positive visualization truly excites me. I began to learn its power when I was young, and it has served me well for many years, particularly after I figured out that I could use it for anything important to me. At present, I work with people in different sports and other enterprises and help them learn how to reprogram their minds to see and approach the things they would really like to have happen. It is a great venue for creativity, by the way. You can do all kinds of things to simulate the experience you are going to have.

For instance, if I work with a quarterback and our focus is on playing cool and within himself in a pressure situation, I play crowd noises through speakers. I get him into his uniform, pads, and helmet. I do all that I can to put him in precisely the situation he will be in so that his RAS will index the visualization and consider it part of his ordinary experience. When the time comes, the pressure will be a small fraction of what it would have been otherwise. He will have fought that battle several times already and with a positive outcome.

As you think about visualizing what can be in your life, here are some practical steps you can take:

- *Pray about your goals.* Here already is one difference between my idea of visualization and the popular self-help idea. I have no interest in think-and-grow-rich schemes or anything motivated by selfishness. A follower of Jesus Christ should always want to function within God's will. So the very first thing you should do is pray and pray regularly about the direction you see yourself heading. Obviously, there are some goals you don't need to wonder about. It's unnecessary to ask God whether or not you should be trying to do your best at your job. That's a no-brainer; we are to do everything with excellence. You don't need to ask God if he wants you to be a better spouse or parent; obviously, that is his desire. But if you want to start your own business or meet the right husband or wife with whom to share your life, these are matters you need to put before God in prayer so that the bottom-line authority for your actions isn't even in your brain but in heaven. "May my meditation be sweet to Him; I will be glad in the LORD" (Psalm 104:34).

- *Clarify your goals.* Most of us aren't nearly as clear on what we want to do and where we want to go as we think we are. There are people who feel a vague urge to launch off in a different career direction, but they have also given consideration to becoming full-time missionaries, and then they have had thoughts about staying in their current line of work but striving for promotion. It is not helpful to feed mixed signals into our subconscious minds, is it? As you pray about your goals, clarify them as well. Be absolutely sure about precisely where you are heading. I recommend that you sit down and write yourself a mission statement for life. Yes, I know. Many of us are reluctant to spend time on things like that. But reflecting on what that statement is, concentrating on finding precisely the right words, seeing your hand write them out, and then reading back what you've written can be a powerful visual exercise in itself. You make the idea real by giving it a physical form.

    Write it. Read it. Read it again—aloud. Read it again, aloud and with confidence. Read it to your family and then your close friends. Do all these things to make your ideas tangible goals, instead of some wispy dream that you keep locked in an old closet in the back of your brain.

Bringing your goals out into the open, then shining the light on them, is the first step toward being able to visualize them really coming to pass.

- *Visualize your goals regularly.* The power of visualization comes through repetition, just like regular practice. Dramatic studies have proven that we can get muscle benefit simply by visualizing athletic actions without actually practicing them. How can that be possible? Again, your RAS doesn't differentiate between real and imaginary. It sends the same impulses to your body through visualization that it would if you were really acting. Therefore, you will want to conduct your mental rehearsals regularly and frequently, just as you would if you were practicing the piano or a golf shot. I heard recently about a young man who broke both his arms but didn't want to waste time while he was in bed recuperating. He had a typewriter keyboard placed in front of him, and for weeks he stared at the keyboard and imagined his fingers on the right keys. He mentally typed words and sentences and paragraphs without ever moving his arms, and when the casts were taken off, he typed for the first time in his life—at a speed of thirty words per minute. His hands had been learning and accumulating a kind of false body memory. Needless to say, if he could have combined his mental practice with physical practice, his speed would have been even better. But this shows how powerful the mind can be, even alone. Use regular, scheduled concentration.

- *Visualize your goals in fine detail.* When I mentally rehearsed my thousands of fistfights, I didn't just see myself standing over some defeated opponent. That wouldn't have been particularly helpful. No, I threw every punch in my mind. I got my feet in the right position. I placed my body in the best possible location that the room had to offer, and I countered the different kinds of punches and attacks that I could imagine coming from my opponent. Then, during those thirty or so occasions when the fight actually happened, there was nothing my opponent could do without my subconscious mind thinking, *Been there, done that.* This point is so important. What if you are afraid to go into your boss's office and ask for that raise? You visualize it in detail, imagining everything he might say because now is the time to figure out exactly what a good, positive response to his comments might be. You think about how you might become defensive or say the wrong thing, and you prepare yourself now so that it won't happen. Mental preparation in advance can help us keep our cool, be at our best, and come up with those great lines we often wish we had said, after it is too late. Whatever it is that you want to do, play the mind games in advance, and play them in slow motion and with several different alternate endings. You will be making the whole situation an everyday reality for your inner thoughts.

• *Visualize the celebration.* How is it going to feel when you cross the finish line? What will your emotions be like? Go into detail, just as you have done for the execution of this feat. When we do this, we energize ourselves. We hear the sizzle, we smell the steak, and our stomachs begin to growl. (You see, those words alone made you a little hungry, didn't they?) An example of how this works in the emotional sense is found in Philippians 2. Paul is telling us to take on the mind-set of Christ—that is, one of pure humility. He describes the humility that Christ showed in being God yet being willing to put on human flesh and suffering the consequences. Then he describes the celebration that will occur because Christ has been willing to submit himself to these things:

But he gave up his place with God and made himself nothing. He was born as a man and became like a servant. And when he was living as a man, he humbled himself and was fully obedient to God, even when that caused his death—death on a cross. So God raised him to the highest place. God made his name greater than every other name so that every knee will bow to the name of Jesus—everyone in heaven, on earth, and under the earth. And everyone will confess that Jesus Christ is Lord and bring glory to God the Father. (Philippians 2:7–11 NCV)

Note the visual language of these words. We see Christ on earth as a servant, then accepting the horrible fate of crucifixion—every first-century reader knew what that looked like. Then we see God "raising him to the highest place" and all of creation bowing at the knee when his name is spoken. Paul included people, angels, and demons in this word picture. That is powerful detail. For centuries this passage has inspired people to worship God, and I believe it is because the language is so visual and also so celebratory. It has sizzle. We see the connection between being humble now and being rewarded in heaven later. (Of course, no knees will bow before us; Paul's point is that we should be motivated to imitate the attitude of Christ.)

- *Take action.* The most powerful visualization is the kind that is combined with real action. Looking back at the Russian Olympic athletes mentioned earlier, the group that excelled was the one that undertook a large amount of positive mental rehearsal and a reasonable amount of physical practice. No matter how much you tell yourself you can be successful at some pursuit, at some point you have to do something concrete with your body in the real world. That does not mean quitting your job prematurely if some new career is your goal. It does not mean rushing anything before its time. It does mean getting off the fence and taking some kind of positive action to reinforce the mental encouragement you are building.

* *Use props.* Remember, we are talking about being visual. Not all of it needs to occur inside your mind. Use visible props of all kinds to remind yourself to keep focusing on what you want to happen. You can write your goals on a note card and keep it in plain sight. You can display photographs or images that depict what you want to achieve. Place props in critical locations so that you remember not to let your passion fade before moving on to something else. Rome wasn't built in a day, and your mind—which is much more glorious and detailed and complex than Rome—won't be changed in a day or week either.

VISUALIZING GODLINESS

Finally, I want to say a word about how this idea can be a power-based principle in your spiritual life. We don't often think of visualization in these terms—too many people turn it to self-centered, materialistic ends—but I have already demonstrated that visualization is a biblical and godly principle.

God wants us to have new, positive minds that are drenched with the sweet scent of heaven. Listen to what he says about the way we should treat his scriptural principles: "Teach them to your children, and talk about them when you sit at home and walk along the road, when you lie down and when you get up. Write them down and tie them to your hands as a sign. Tie them on your forehead to remind you" (Deuteronomy 6:7–8 NCV).

Those are pretty practical action points, wouldn't you say? We are being taught to fill all our perceptions, all our experiences with God's truth and to teach it to our children as well. He is showing us how to use godliness props.

In the New Testament we have Paul's idea of mental transformation: "Do not be shaped by this world; instead be changed within by a new way of thinking. Then you will be able to decide what God wants for you; you will know what is good and pleasing to him and what is perfect" (Romans 12:2 NCV). Again we see the idea that your mind does not exist in a vacuum. Your mind is going to take one form or another. The world will try to fit your thinking into a certain mold so that you'll be just like everyone else.

God, however, wants you to be "changed within by a new way of thinking." The Holy Spirit is working within every believer, making him or her a little bit more like the image of Christ every single day. But we have an incredible influence on how fast or how slow that happens. We can actually become obstacles to the positive transformation the Spirit wants for us, or we can participate by filling our minds with the godly things that help us become those redeemed, Christlike individuals we are meant to be.

We can also use visualization as a very powerful aid to prayer. For example, try making Psalm 23 your prayer, visualizing all the images David used there: God makes you to lie down in green pastures; he leads you beside the still waters. Can you see that? Feel the breeze and the presence of the Good Shepherd beside you. The beautiful words and delightful images will relax you and help you encounter God in a new way. As you pray for other people, see their faces in your mind. Offer images to God instead of just words, and you will feel more power in your prayer.

You can visualize better relationships too. If your marriage is struggling, spend time beginning to practice a better relationship in your mind. Can you imagine doing that? When you don't *feel* like being loving and kind toward your mate, go off and pray for him or her. Ask for God to help you love your partner, to show you what your marriage should look like: a loving, devoted relationship of two people God has brought together. Visualize yourself being kind, giving gifts, and graciously serving your spouse. See in your mind the very best memories that the two of you have and relive them in detail. Then when you and your spouse are together, you will find a radical improvement in your ability to be the kind of mate God wants you to be.

Finally, ask God to open the eyes of your heart to things as they really are—not simply what they can be but how they already are. There is a wonderful story in the Old Testament, found in 2 Kings 6. The prophet Elisha (the more famous prophet Elijah was his mentor) was in a city surrounded by the hostile army of Syria. His servant became frantic and wondered what should be done. Elisha told him not to fear, for "those who are with us are more than those who are with them" (v. 16).

Those are fine words. But then he gave something far more powerful than a verbal assurance. He asked God to open the eyes of his servant, and it happened. The servant looked around him again and saw that the surrounding mountains were filled with angelic warriors and chariots of fire. They had been there all along, but only the person of true vision could have seen them.

Are you a person of true vision? Ask God to open your eyes that you may see the possibilities that extend your horizon in every direction. It is so tempting to live in the negative essence of superficial appearances as most people do. The economic climate is tough. The world is becoming a dark place. There are so many reasons to feel the despair of Elisha's servant. We need to know that the forces that accompany us are greater than the forces that oppose us. That is a promise that echoes throughout the Scriptures. We are told that we can do all things through Christ, and we are told that he will give us his presence and power. We are promised that Christ has come to overcome the world. We need to open our eyes and visualize that, not because it can be but because it already is.

Seeing is believing for some people, but for others believing is seeing.

Believe and then begin to see what can be. Practice the discipline of positive visualization in your relationships, your faith, your career, and every aspect of who you are. It will mark the beginning of your liberation from the mundane and your entrance to the realm of incredible achievement.

5

....

Belief: Defy the Skeptics

Don't stop me if you think you have heard this one. Seriously.

And if you haven't heard this one, you have been living in a cave since birth. This is a very old and well-known story, but you are about to hear it again—with one difference. I want you to watch someone else. Not the hero, not the villain. This time, keep your eyes on the supporting cast, and you will hear this story as if for the first time.

Maybe you have seen a football game on film, but a blocker is circled on your TV screen rather than the quarterback; normally we follow the ball, but sometimes there is a lot to learn by taking a look at what happens in the background.

I am going to retell the story of David and Goliath, but this time, don't watch the ball. Widen your focus and notice what everyone else on David's team is doing. You see, David had an abundance of highly qualified teammates all around him, but unfortunately, they chose not to step onto the field of play.

The original version of this story is found in 1 Samuel 17, and it has become the ultimate icon of taking on overwhelming opposition. Actually, the Bible has any number of accounts with the same theme: Gideon's small squad defeating a massive army, Moses and the Israelites defying the Egyptian empire, Daniel taming the lion, even eleven disciples overcoming the Roman world with the message of the gospel. So this principle of facing the giants is hardwired into the Scriptures.

The question is, what are the secrets of doing that? The first is clear and obvious: *trust God*. That is the bottom-line essential: "I can do all things through Christ who strengthens me" (Philippians 4:13).

But you also need to believe in the raw materials God has given you and ignore the skeptics. Naysayers are everywhere, and they never keep quiet. Pay attention to them in this version of David's story.

You probably remember that the Israelites had developed a bitter rivalry with the Philistines and were taking a substantial beating. This enemy had a way of creating perpetual headaches for God's people. For example, the Bible tells us that the Philistines cut off the roads by which Israel needed to import iron so they could modernize their weaponry. On one occasion after David had become king, the Philistines succeeded in stealing the ark of the covenant, the most precious treasure the nation owned. The Philistines made life miserable for the chosen people, and they were the number-one reason why the people of God began clamoring for a king.

Then there was Goliath of Gath. He was the ultimate fighting machine, measuring in at a height of over nine feet. By the way, archaeologists have discovered amazingly tall skeletons in Palestine dating to the same period, so don't think we are reading a *tall* tale.

I will let the Bible itself give you an idea of the impression Goliath made on a battlefield:

> He had a bronze helmet on his head, and he was armed with a coat of mail, and the weight of the coat was five thousand shekels of bronze. And he had bronze armor on his legs and a bronze javelin between his shoulders. Now the staff of his spear was like a weaver's beam, and his iron spearhead weighed six hundred shekels; and a shield-bearer went before him. (1 Samuel 17:5–7)

From my years of working in college football, I can tell you that nearly every team has at least one ridiculously impressive human specimen who is the king of the weight room. He is tall, has chiseled muscles, and is built like an oak tree. It is a football truism that the coaches want him to be the first guy off the bus during road games—that is, they want the opponent to get a load of this guy before seeing anything else.

Goliath was Philistia's first player off the bus. He would thunder over to the front lines, his armor clanging as he walked, and trash-talk the opposition. He challenged them: "Hey, Israel, hit me with your best shot! Send me one warrior, and we'll go head to head. If he can whip me, we'll come over there and be your slaves—every one of us. But if your guy goes down, then you have to be our slaves. Let's get it on, winner take all!"

Israel had some pretty good soldiers, but when the call went out for volunteers, not one of them stepped forward. The Bible says they were "dismayed" (v. 11).

BEWARE THE WRATH OF THE DELIVERY BOY

Then somebody's little brother showed up. He was a skinny teenager, fifteen years old and not even battle trained. David's job was to stay home and look after the sheep. He also wrote poetry and played a harp. Think of David as the water boy.

As a matter of fact, that is exactly what he was doing on this day. Jesse, his dad, had given him some sacks of groceries and said, "Take those to your older brothers. Also, see if you can pick up any inside information on the war effort."

David had three brothers stationed in the Valley of Elah, where the Philistines were driving them backward every day. David was delivering lunch. It was bread and cheese, actually, so apparently they were eating cheese sandwiches though mayo is not mentioned.

As the shepherd boy was on his way, he heard this giant bellowing his insults, really offensive stuff, against the people of God. David could not figure out why everyone was putting up with that loudmouth. He quickly dropped off the sack of groceries with one of the guards and then hustled up to the front lines to pick up some news on the battle for his dad.

David saw his brothers all in battle garb, taking their positions. Suddenly, Goliath came out from his tent, and that was all it took for the Israelites to scatter like bugs from a displaced rock. That's the kind of thing that simply did not register on David's mental grid. You see, David wasn't as harmless as he looked. One day while he was composing poetry, he had been trying to think of something that rhymed with *Zion*. He was suddenly confronted with, of all things, a *lion*. He killed the beast and got the word he was looking for, all in one fell swoop.

Another time he was strumming his harp, and the music apparently attracted a bear. The bear, too, went down.

David may have been a shepherd, but he had the heart of a warrior. When David looked at the annoying windbag from Gath, he saw a problem no greater than a bear or a lion. He couldn't imagine all those soldiers showing their taillights; why not deal with the pest so everyone could enjoy their sandwiches in peace?

David followed the soldiers and asked, "Who does that meathead think he is?"

I wonder if what he really wanted to ask the soldiers was, "Who do you guys think *you* are?" That's the real issue, isn't it? What do we believe about ourselves, about our God-given talents and abilities? Proverbs 23:7 comes to mind, telling us, "For as he thinks within himself, so he is" (NASB).

The soldiers circled around the shepherd and started describing all the great gifts and prizes that would be awarded to anyone capable of knocking off Goliath—the victor would be given gold and the king's daughter as a bride, and he would never have to pay taxes. That's in verse 25—you can look it up. Kill the giant, win the lottery.

At this point one of David's brothers walked up, saw David, and rolled his eyes. "What are you doing here, little brother?" he said. "Don't you usually hang out with the sheep? Or have you come to watch the big boys do battle?"

For David, it was hard to tell the big boys from the sheep on this battleground. Saul, the king, got wind of all this talk and sent for the shepherd boy. David went to the king and told him, "Nobody should be losing sleep over this Goliath fellow. Let me go fight him."

Saul told him that was crazy talk. "He'll eat you in one bite," said the king. "You're just a kid, and he was mangling whole regiments when you were in diapers."

David told him about the lion and the bear, and Saul must have thought,

This kid is not smart enough to be afraid. But to David it made no difference whether he was facing lions, bears, or giants because he knew that the issue is not who you think the other guy is but who you think *you* are.

I realize we tend to save this story for the children, but it fires me up. We are the ones—those of us on the retreat from the front lines of life—who need to study David's youth. All of us are facing giants these days.

We face the giant of the job market, the giant task of holding a family together, the giant obstacles blocking us from reaching our goals—but most of us are a lot more like David's brothers than David himself. We should be saying, "You know, I've already beaten problem after problem through God's power and blessing. Why would this problem be any different?"

But we don't believe. And we're surrounded by teammates who are talking themselves and others out of the game. This is why I told you to watch the people in the background; even the king gave David reasons why he was bound to fail.

WHO DO YOU THINK YOU ARE?

Here is the key to understanding what made David special: he trusted in God, but he also believed in the skills God had given him.

He went to a dry creek bed and picked up five smooth stones. Then he untied his sling from around his shoulder and gave it a sharp pull to test its strength. What you need to know is that this was the perfect choice of a weapon. Shepherds were very handy with slings; it was how they protected their flock, but soldiers used them too. Israelite warriors from the house of Benjamin were known for being able to sling a stone equally well with their left hand and their right—we are told they could fire a stone at a velocity of one hundred miles per hour, to a distance of almost a hundred yards. The smoother the stone, the better it would fly. So go ahead and discard those images in your mind of a child's slingshot. This was a formidable weapon, and Goliath knew all about it.

So David chose his weapon wisely. He found the tool that bridged the gap between a shepherd and a soldier. Then the Bible tells us he *ran* to meet the giant. That word excites me every time I study this narrative. A teenager with no combat training whatsoever is on his way to take on the world heavy-weight champ. But he doesn't creep toward the fight with trembling and tentative steps. *He sprints!* He believes in God, he believes in his ability, and he has chosen his weapon. He is a man of action, even at fifteen. I believe this is also a great lesson in how we deal with adversity in our lives. Goliath represented adversity, and David ran to meet him head-on. The retail company that coined the phrase "No Fear" during the nineties just might have had David in mind.

Again, let's take a peek at the supporting cast. Though the Bible doesn't fill in the picture for us, we can figure it out on our own. Can't you guess what the cowering Israelites were thinking as they watched this spectacle? These were big, battle-hardened GIs wearing full armor, and they were hiding in the bushes, watching a little guy in a leather jumpsuit rush the Incredible Hulk!

The king had said, "If you are really going through with this thing, you might as well wear my armor. It is top-of-the-line, and I won't be using it."

David had said, "No thanks. It is way too big, and I won't need it anyway." David planned on taking the offensive. Playing defense is an exercise in futility when the guy across the line from you weighs four times your weight. You have to believe in yourself and go on the attack.

The Israelites were playing defense, and they were playing it a little farther back every day. Eventually, there would have been no Israel to play it in. So you can imagine their body language, which reflected their constant readiness to retreat.

You can just hear someone shouting, "Hey, look over there—it's the delivery boy!"

Someone else shouts back, "What, the kid with the sandwiches? What about him?"

"That wacky kid is going after the big guy—he's running right at Goliath with a full head of steam! No foolin'!"

That makes everyone look up. Suddenly there's pushing and shoving on the front line. Every man wants to get a better view of this crazy stunt on the battlefield. But by the time they have jostled to get in position to see what's happening, it's all over.

"What happened? Where did the giant go?"

"He went down! The kid nailed him with a fastball—right between the eyes!"

"What? Impossible!"

"Man, I never thought a kid would take him down. That was the last thing that entered my mind."

"Last thing that entered Goliath's too—if you catch my drift!"

With that (at least the way I'm imagining what happened), everybody has a good laugh, and suddenly, there is nothing to fear anymore. They raise a great cry, start chanting, "Delivery boy! Delivery boy!" and charge after the Philistines, looking like Mel Gibson's men in *Braveheart*. And it's Israel with the upset.

That is one of the great things about courage—it rubs off. You can have an army of people doing nothing, and suddenly, when one leader steps up, they become an army capable of doing nearly anything. But isn't it kind of sad that it took a fifteen-year-old shepherd boy to step forward? Wouldn't you have thought that at least one good man might seize the day in God's army? Yes, I understand that this was God's plan for a kind of coming-out party for David. But we often miss the point that David did what any man in that regiment—*any* man—could just as easily have done. The times were not waiting for the right man. They were waiting for any man with the right attitude.

Those five smooth stones were available to anyone who wanted to pick them up, and the sling was a weapon that many of those men had already mastered. A number of them probably had more skill than David.

So what was their excuse? They lacked one ingredient: a belief in themselves.

THE MUMBLE OF THE CROWD

Have you ever wondered why, in an old Western film, the hero always comes riding out of the wilderness? There is always a town filled with people who are being intimidated by some outlaw, but the guy in the white hat comes into town and makes short work of him before riding off into the sunset again. Why can't the townsfolk do it themselves?

The problem is that these people spend too much time hanging out in that old saloon and psyching each other out so that nothing gets done. That is exactly what happened with the soldiers who were afraid of Goliath.

Let's detour and review another familiar story in which the same thing happened. As the Israelites were traveling to the wonderful land God had promised them, Moses sent out scouts to find out what it was like. When these scouts returned, two of them (Joshua and Caleb) raved about the beauty and bounty of this incredible region. Their recommendation: "Let's go get it!"

But the other scouts could only talk about the tribes already occupying the land. If you read Numbers 13, you see that every time they opened their mouths, they made the obstacles larger. Finally they said, "There we saw the giants . . . and we were like grasshoppers in our own sight, and so we were in their sight" (v. 33).

This group, which made up the majority, had talked itself into being terrified of the giants they saw. They even admitted that they, the scouts, had become grasshoppers in their own eyes! That's what we do to ourselves when we share our fear.

Worse, they spread their fear to the whole nation of Israel so that entering the promised land could not happen for forty years. The price of their self-doubt was that the whole generation would die in the wilderness when their problem could have been solved in the same way that David would solve Israel's problem many years later—by stepping out in faith.

Back in 1 Samuel 17 you may have noticed that David asked the soldiers what could be won by the man who defeated the giant. That was the way his mind worked: he was an *upside* guy who thought in terms of rewards rather than risks. The soldiers told him about all kinds of wonderful prizes, and David had to question, "If this is true, why aren't you guys out there competing to see who slays the giant?"

The reason they weren't out there was because they had been staring at that helmet, that spear, and that armor and listening to all that trash-talking for too long. Then they became their own echo chamber until they became grasshoppers in their own eyes. They gave themselves time to get a good fear going, and fear is contagious. When we hang around fearful people, their fear rubs off on us.

David had been around only sheep lately, which had given him a lot of time to talk to God. And those poems he wrote were about the greatness and the providence of God; he used his harp to set them to music. He practiced the principle we've already discussed—filling the mind with powerful, positive, and godly things. So by the time David came riding out of the wilderness, he couldn't understand all the negative talk. It was everywhere! He saw it in the soldiers first. Then his brother walked up to him and started speaking through layers of sarcasm, attempting to cut him even further down to size. Even the king, the highest authority, had a gloomy outlook. Friend, family, kings—this was a contagion of can't, but David was immune. I think God kept him out in the field because it is better to hear the bleating of sheep than the whining of cowards. In the silence we can hear from God; in the crowd his voice can be drowned out by moaning.

The Bible tells us that all it took was one well-placed stone to the giant's head, and the dam broke—the same frightened Hebrew soldiers had one of their greatest victories. Just like that, the Israelites went on a rampage. Did God suddenly give them the power? No, they had it all along. What they didn't have was confidence in themselves and in God's will for them.

How often do we listen to the crowd and its negative prospect of the world? Sometimes we laugh at young people who have not yet gotten the memo about what is supposed to be impossible. We mistake their courage for foolishness and our fear for wisdom. We let those around us define who we are by what they see as our limitations rather than our abilities.

When he became king, David established an elite corps of warriors known as David's Mighty Men, a band of brothers who routinely outfought lions, Philistines, and massive numbers of other soldiers. They were the Bible's superheroes. Yet these were the same underachievers from the Valley of Elah. Now think of that: here were men capable of incredible heroism, champions of Israel, yet if a courageous young man had never come forward, these potential champions would have skulked in the shadows for the rest of their lives.

You have to wonder how much greatness is lying hidden in our society today simply because these men and women of future greatness are surrounded by the negativism of this world. They gobble with the turkeys rather than fly with the eagles.

THE POWER OF YES

David was one of the most talented men portrayed in the entire rich tapestry of Scripture. He was a military genius with a warrior's heart, a poet, a musician, a charismatic political leader, a handsome man, and even a gifted dancer. So how did that happen? Perhaps he simply won the genetic lottery and received all these talents at birth.

I don't think so. Because when I read about David, I read about a man who believed in God and believed in himself. I know a few Davids, people who seem to try all kinds of new things and have no problems mastering them. We make a great mistake when we assume they're simply gifted people, constitutionally unlike us. The most important gift of all is confidence, and that's something that can be attained.

David lived life to the fullest, enjoying a passion for the arts, the pursuit of God, the craft of statesmanship, the depth of friendship (think of his relationship with Jonathan), the joy of romantic love, and the athleticism of dance. But he was painfully human too—the Bible paints a blunt portrait of his failings, particularly later in life. He was just as capable of failure as any of us, but he achieved great things because he set out with confidence to achieve them.

We have looked at the characters in the background. We looked at the villain, then the hero. Now let's look at someone else: *you*. That is our real subject, isn't it? As you read about the shepherd/king, you were thinking about your own issues with self-belief and courage. As you read about the skeptics and the can't-do crowd, you were thinking of the people in your inner circle. And what have you decided? Are you the one who takes on challenges at a sprint, or do you hang back and murmur about prizes you will never win?

There are eight verses spread out across the Bible that repeat God's all-important foundation for life together in this world: "Love your neighbor as yourself." The first is in Leviticus, four are in the Gospels, two are in Paul's letters, and the final one is in James. That is a double-layered command. The obvious part, on the outside, is that we are to love others. But we can only do so if the inside part, the assumed part—"as [you love] yourself"—is taken care of.

If you've been alive for a while, you have seen how true this is. Those who cannot love themselves will never be successful in loving others. The reason is that love is a power from God, and it cannot be given away without first being received.

God says to you, "I want you to love others. But here is where it starts: accept my love for you. If I can love you, warts and all, there is no reason in the world you can't love yourself." Then when we learn loving self-acceptance, we grow strong in what the psychologists call *ego integrity*. A powerful self-concept frees us to be loving, giving people among others.

FEEDING THE CONFIDENCE OF OTHERS

Think of the people you know who are confident and positive. I don't mean arrogant and cocky—that approach usually masks a low self-image. Truly confident people are actually humble because they understand that to love ourselves is to know ourselves, strengths as well as weaknesses. They know that God has freed them to move forward based on their gifts, and they do not cower under their shortcomings. Think of the self-assured people in your life. You'll agree that they think clearly, they listen well, and they act when it is time to act.

But those of us who do not believe in ourselves are actually failing to think clearly and accurately. There is a problem in that mental grid we keep talking about. Somewhere along the way, we got the idea that we are prone to failure, and failure is painful. Obviously, children who are well loved and encouraged develop strong self-concepts. They are not afraid to risk failure, and they move ahead in confidence—they are the Davids of the world.

Sadly enough, my observation is that such people are in a minority. Too many of us have emerged from childhood with a tendency to avoid risk at all costs. We hear those old parental voices in our heads telling us, "There you go—you messed up again! I told you that would happen. What in the world is wrong with you?" All parents love their children; the sad thing is they fail to realize just how powerful their words are, and they also are not aware that they haven't expressed their love unconditionally.

But let's not lay all the blame at the feet of the world's hardworking, long-suffering parents. There are many voices out there telling us that Goliath is unbeatable. It has been my experience over the years that most people are surrounded by "friends" who place upon them the limitations they have accepted for themselves. If, say, Wanda was divorced after an unsuccessful marriage, she is expecting the same thing to happen in the marriages of her friends. If Bob gets out of school and can't find a job, he tells his buddy, who graduates the next year, "There are no jobs out there. Be ready to be rejected."

This doesn't come from ill intentions; our own bad experiences are so powerful for us that we do not want to see them happen to our friends. But think about young people, who have the whole world before them. What if from the best of intentions we discourage them from thinking outside the box and being creative? Yes, they may well fall flat on their faces, but so what? It is not only a part of life but the part that most helps us to grow.

Let's say Cody is twenty-two years old and has a passion for music. Well, you have all kinds of statistics and information about how next-to-impossible it is to break into the music industry. So you decide to save him the time of pursuing that dream by showering him with reasons why it is not going to work and encouraging him to settle for an entry-level job somewhere. Maybe you convinced him, and Cody goes ahead and finds a job in the mall. The price of that pragmatism is crushing the dream inside of someone—and dreams are the fuel for the hope that makes life worth living.

MY CASE STUDY

Since you know a little about my life, think about the difference a crowd once made for me. I was at a college reunion and mentioned my greatest regret in life—missing my senior year of playing college football. One guy challenged me to go for it. He was a David, wasn't he? The idea to actually play that year at an advanced age wasn't even on the table yet, but he thought outside the box. He saw what was in my eyes and recognized the power of the dream that was still within me—even though I didn't realize that the dream was even attainable.

That is what I call an encourager. I try to be that person for others and help push them toward going after the thing that really makes their eyes light up.

I didn't leave that reunion and immediately start preparing to play. I began researching my eligibility, and I avoided talking to others about the plan forming in my mind. You can imagine what most of them would have said, can't you? A seed of hope had been planted in me, and I had to water that seed and nurture it carefully. Just how many words from naysayers would that seed have survived? I knew that most of the people who cared about me simply wouldn't want me to get my head separated from my body.

Still, there were a number of hurdles that had to be overcome—a squad of Goliaths, each one formidable in its own right. One of them was the skeptical crowd. If they told David he was too young, they would tell me I was too old. Have you ever noticed how it is never the right time, according to people who don't believe?

Those who knew me best—my family and close friends—were a little skeptical, and that was totally understandable. But when they saw I meant business, they got on board. They were wise enough to encourage me rather than crush my spirit.

The others were a different story. They gave every reason why I would fail. As I listened to them carefully, I discovered that they were talking more about themselves than about me. They lumped me in with their own physical problems. "What about knees and hips?" they would point out. "They're more brittle, now that you're fifty-nine years old. How do you think they will hold up under the heavy contact of college football?" Some told me how fast the kids are today and how much bigger they are.

Then there were those who painted pictures in my mind of what it would feel like to be laid up in the hospital because I had pursued a crazy dream when my life was just fine the way it was. After it became clear I was actually going to do this thing, I heard that one guy said, "He's got to be taking growth hormones—that's the only way a guy could do it at his age!" A negative mind-set is a powerful thing for some people. They are so convinced that something is impossible, that when it gets done, they look for smoke and mirrors.

By simply doing something unusual I learned a lot of lessons I never expected. People have self-imposed limitations; therefore, in their minds I must have them too. They could never succeed at this; therefore, I shouldn't even try. Fortunately, I can say that I had enough David in me to plug up my ears and do what I knew with every fiber of my being I could do.

People were asking, "Who do you think you are?" And my reply was, "I think I'm someone capable of achieving an extraordinary goal."

We may or may not hold back other people, but we can certainly hold back ourselves, simply based on who we think we are and what we choose to believe about ourselves. The Bible tells us we can do all things through Christ. It tells us that faith the size of a mustard seed can move a mountain and that prayer accomplishes miracles. I choose to build my self-concept from those promises rather than from any failures in my past.

YOUR CASE STUDY

But enough about me. Let's get back to you.

What have you decided about yourself based on these words? When we talk about the Goliaths of this world, what is that a metaphor for in your life? In other words, what is the giant that looms on your horizon? I want you to stop for a moment and think about that. It is important to realize just what it is because the truth is that life isn't a battle in which we hold our ground. At any moment we are either moving forward or moving backward. David's friends had been moving backward for a long time, and there was only one way that could end. David moved forward in a sprint, and his country's greatest crisis was over in the matter of an instant.

You can charge, or you can retreat, but standing still for very long is not an option—life is change, and the human engine left in neutral will cease to run.

If you are willing to admit that you are in slow-retreat mode, the next question is, what's holding you back? I want to suggest to you that the problem is a lack of belief: you really don't think you can do it.

In his book *Hide or Seek*, Dr. James Dobson described his mental image of a person with low self-esteem. You're walking down a road, and you cross the path of a weary traveler. He looks really tired and discouraged, and you see that his fist grips something he is holding across his shoulder. You ask, "What have you got there?" And he just looks very sad. You walk behind him and take a good look, discovering that this fellow is carrying a chain that must be a mile long. Connected to the chain are chunks of scrap iron; bits of old, busted tires; and little items of garbage of every variety. It smells awful.

You take a closer look and see that each piece of rubbish, large or small, bears a tag with an inscription telling about some disappointment, humiliation, rejection, or failure that the weary traveler has experienced in the past. After reading a few of the tags, you feel really sad and wish you hadn't looked.

"So why are you dragging this chain?" you ask. "Can't you just drop it and walk away?"

"No," says the traveler. "It's a part of me."

"But that doesn't make any sense," you say. "All you have to do is just open your hand, let go, and be on your way. You won't believe how much easier it will be to walk."

But for some reason you can't convince this fellow. He just trudges on, leaving deep ruts in the road that spread the traces of his failure wherever he goes.[1]

If you think it is irrational to drag an unnecessary chain through life, you are right. And it makes just as little sense to carry a mind-set of past failures into the fresh road of your future. All you need to do is let go.

Try this exercise. Take a sheet of paper and draw the chain you would be dragging. Just make a simple line going from one corner of the page to the opposite corner. Then list a few of the events that could contribute to a negative outlook if you dwelled upon them.

Then look at each of these items and ask yourself, "Is there any reason this event can't be over for good in my life, starting right now?" And with a stroke of your pen, cut it off the chain.

Sure, this is just an exercise on paper. Call it silly or meaningless if you want as long as you realize that the real power is always inside your own mind. In an earlier chapter we discussed replacing negative subconscious signals with positive ones. If you want to travel light, if you want to be able to sprint toward the things you most want in life, you have to find some way to know you are finally leaving the past behind. Your past only has the power you give it.

Unlike God, we don't have selective memories. We can't just choose to not recall our past—at least not easily. But we can disconnect these recollections from the power socket of present decisions. What would your life look like if you could turn off the old static and walk away from every negative influence that has been hampering your journey?

That's the first half of the equation. You have to walk away from the influences that damaged your self-image because any damage was done wrongfully. This brings us to the second thing you must do, which is to begin building a positive self-concept. Let's take a look at how that can be done.

TOWARD HEALTHY SELF-LOVE

There is no easy formula for loving yourself, but let me describe what it looks like. In an issue of the *Hope Health Letter*, Nathaniel Branden suggested that you can tell if you have high self-esteem if you:

* have a sense of humor
* are open to new ideas and experiences
* project an attitude of flexibility and inventiveness
* preserve harmony and dignity under stress
* speak and move with ease and spontaneity
* are comfortable giving and receiving compliments and affection
* can speak honestly about accomplishments and shortcomings[2]

If you consider this to be a checklist, how would you grade yourself on each of these?

Let me suggest that you begin to understand how God thinks about you. According to the Bible, he knew you long before you were ever born. He had a plan for bringing you into the world and giving you a significant mission for your time here. "For we are His workmanship, created in Christ Jesus for good works, which God prepared beforehand that we should walk in them" (Ephesians 2:10).

When he made you, he gave you custom fingerprints. Have you ever thought about that? Your DNA, your mind, your gifts, and your destiny match those of no one else who has ever lived or who ever will. God doesn't produce cheap merchandise; everything he creates is the best it could possibly be, and the truth is that his children are the crown of his creation—the things he loves most.

God loves you so much that if you were the only person who ever lived, he still would have sent his Son to die for you. He loves you so much that there is no moment when he is not watching you, calling to you, and craving your intimate fellowship. Have you ever thought about that? No matter how many people, because of their own bruises and limitations, have led you to believe bad things about yourself, the creator of this universe wants nothing more than to know you and guide you now and then to have you as his guest in heaven for all eternity. He loves you with an everlasting love, and there is actually nothing you can do about that. He will continue loving you and pursuing you no matter what.

When Jesus left this earth, he said that he had to go so that he could prepare a special place for us and that his house has many mansions. That is our destiny, and this life is about growing toward it. Yes, that growth process requires all kinds of bumps and bends in the road. Sometimes there is incredible pain, even heartbreak. But each of these things will become raw material for the wise, mature version of you that he is building even now. The tough parts are supposed to become not stumbling blocks but stepping-stones toward a better life.

Most of all, keep this in mind: the unpleasant items on that chain behind you—if you are still dragging it—are things that he doesn't even see. When Jesus Christ died on the cross, his perfect, spotless righteousness was exchanged for every sin you will ever commit. It is all forgiven—past, present, and future. God separated us from our sin, the Bible says, as far as the west is separated from the east. As far as he is concerned, there *is* no chain. If God himself will not hold your past against you, is there any reason why you yourself should?

Now, look at all that he has given you. Go to a good counselor and take a test to discover your best aptitudes if you don't already know them. What is your personality type? Don't dwell on who you are not, but be thankful to God for who you really are because I guarantee you there is no person on the face of this earth who doesn't have unique gifts and talents from God and a personalized mission designed to give him or her joy.

Finally, look for a circle of encouragers. In many churches today it's possible to get involved in a good home fellowship and Bible study group—or, at the very least, a good Sunday morning adult class. Build the relationships in that group, encourage others there, and allow them to encourage you. At the same time, if you can detect a crowd of skeptics, people who tend to remind you of your limitations, cut off their influence. That does not mean they can't be your friends. Some of them may even be family, and you must continue to love and support them. Just do not give them the power to hold you back.

With the chain now discarded and fading into the shadows behind you and the goal out before you, why not take off and run? I don't mean that you should be frantic and throw caution to the wind or do anything that is reckless or poorly thought out. But pick up the pace a little bit. Begin to take positive steps toward that passion, the dream that energizes you.

Believe in yourself, forget the skeptics, and go for it. And guess what? As David discovered, you are likely to look back and see them following at your heels, chanting your name, and finally chasing after their own long-denied goals. Seeing that feels very good.

So let me ask you: Who do you think you are?

6
....

Commitment:
Move Forward Relentlessly

The young man had a rough childhood. His father beat him regularly and told him he had no brains. The boy had few friends and struggled to stay in school. Counselors told him that if he was going to have any hope of making a living, he should learn some kind of mechanical skill.

The young man decided to try the acting profession, but he couldn't seem to make an impression. He played a few bit parts in low-budget films, but his career could get no traction. The only thing he could call his own was his collections of struggles; maybe, he decided, he could find a way to write about them. Later he would say, "Success is usually the culmination of controlling failure."

One night in 1975, he found just the vehicle he was looking for. The young man watched the world heavyweight boxing champion defend his title on television. Muhammad Ali was the champion, and the challenger was Chuck Wepner, a consummate underdog.

He found the scenario inspiring: an obscure boxer climbing into the ring to challenge the greatest fighter of the century. The fight went the full fifteen rounds, and at the end Wepner was still standing—a proud accomplishment considering the odds against him.

The young man sat and thought about what he had just watched. There was something more than a prizefight here. It was the little guy refusing to live little. In other words, David was answering Goliath's call one more time. The failed actor, whose name was Sylvester Stallone, identified with Wepner, seeing his own audacity reflected in the fighter's struggle. He sensed that Wepner's story could touch some deep chord within millions of other people as well.

Stallone sat down and wrote a script, calling it *Rocky*. For the first time in his life, he knew he had come across something special, something he could leverage into his big break. He committed himself mind, body, and soul to the idea.

His instincts were solid. United Artists was enthusiastic about producing the film, but they saw it as a vehicle for an established star in the lead. Robert Redford, Burt Reynolds, James Caan, and Ryan O'Neal were all considered to play the lead role of Rocky. The presence of a blockbuster star would also mean more money and a bigger production, which in turn would guarantee box office success.

What's not to like about that? If you'd written the script, how quickly would you have said yes? Your script—sold to a major Hollywood studio with a matinee idol playing your role.

Stallone didn't see it that way and held out. He saw himself in the lead even though he was an obscure and unproven actor competing with the big boys. That was as crazy as Rocky taking on Apollo Creed in the movie. Stallone might have scared the filmmakers away. But this was *his* dream, *his* vision, and he politely explained why he should play the part. He won over the producers.

Rocky was filmed on a tight budget of just over one million dollars. It made more than one hundred times that at the box office, won three Oscars, including Best Picture, and thrust Stallone into the upper echelon of Hollywood's elite. The movie is still considered a classic, the iconic underdog movie that has inspired a thousand imitations.

Imagine that level of commitment. Stallone believed in himself for years when no one else did. Then he believed so firmly in the power of his dream that he could say, "I can play this role better than Redford—and I am willing to do it even without the big budget." He stood firm in the presence of the powerful because his power base was a dream to which he had fully committed.

Have you ever believed in anything with that kind of total assurance? Like his boxer, Stallone went the distance. I wonder how many of us are willing to take the big risks and pay the big prices.

Let's take you, for example. Think about your greatest dream; just name it in your head right now, or say it out loud. What is the one goal that would thrill you the most if you achieved it?

Now on the heels of that question, answer this one: What price would you be willing to pay to make that dream become reality? By payment, I don't mean anything financial; I mean sweat equity. How much personal comfort would you willingly give up in order to step closer to your vision?

A farmer tells me he overheard a pig and a chicken having this conversation. The chicken said, "I'm fully committed to giving a dozen eggs a day."

The pig scoffed, "A dozen eggs? That's not commitment, that's participation! Giving bacon, now, *that's* total commitment."

Great goals come at great cost. Another word for that is *sacrifice*. In this chapter we are going to think about what that would mean in your life and for your dream.

WISHES AND DREAMS

Let's define our terms. A dream is a goal that you're willing to purchase at a significant cost to yourself. It might well involve a lifetime commitment.

A wish, on the other hand, is a fleeting fantasy.

There is a big difference. Consider a roomful of people—let's say the sanctuary of a church. In that room there are as many wishes and dreams as there are noses. Your pastor has a vision of tripling the size of his congregation, ministering to more people in town, and supporting a few more missionaries overseas.

In the second row of the choir, that young lady with the nice smile dreams of writing and recording her own songs. She envisions herself performing in concert at Carnegie Hall.

And see the guy sitting right behind her? He's in middle management at a consulting firm, but every single day of his life, he thinks about what it would be like to have his own business.

Oh, and don't forget the teenager in the back pew; he sees himself growing up to create incredible new video games—or maybe filming the next *Rocky*. Younger people haven't heard the word *no* much yet. Their dreams are often bigger and more scattered. Today it may be professional sports; tomorrow, inventor of the first flying car.

I often tell young people to write those dreams onto their hearts in pencil, not indelible ink; dreams, you see, evolve over time. We may pursue them for years, and once caught, they will look entirely different than we imagined when we first started the chase—but we will know they are the substance of what we have dreamed for all along.

But that full-throttled pursuit, that extra dose of want-to, is what makes the difference between wishes and dreams. You could say that wishes are dreams on the layaway plan; we have to start making payments at some point, or our name will be taken off the tag.

So what is your greatest vision for your life? Each one of us sees some kind of castle-in-the-sky in our mind's eye. The question is, who is willing to start building a stairway to reach it?

We dreamers tend to do one of two things: we either begin to take small steps to make our dreams come true, or we just go on living without getting started. In the latter case the wish begins to fade. At best it becomes a fantasy, no more likely than me flapping my arms and soaring above the treetops.

How many people out there believe they have one great book in them but never get past the first paragraph? At some point you cross an invisible line from potential accomplishment to harmless fantasy.

One of my pleasures in life is music. I enjoy hearing a really skilled and gifted artist perform. I even love watching the focus and concentration on the face of the performer. But I have seen people who don't seem to appreciate the price that has been paid for that ability. At a party they might walk up to a really fine pianist and say, "Wow, you can really play that thing! You just have the gift. I wish I could do that, but I can't even play 'Chopsticks'!" Then they will laugh and move to another conversation.

Musicians may be a little annoyed by such comments. Sure, they know the words were offered with the best of intentions. But the implication was that the musical skill is a gift, like a present handed to them—a talent they are lucky to have, rather than something that came at the price of untold hours of grueling practice.

When musicians are told "I wish I could do that, but I can't," they would love to respond, "Of course you can't. Because you made other choices while I was sacrificing my time and energy for this very moment! Don't wish for what I have unless you are willing to spend fifteen or twenty years making yourself *lucky*."

The Bible says this about dreams and wishes: "For the dream comes through much effort and the voice of a fool through many words" (Ecclesiastes 5:3 NASB). The dreamer works while the fool yaps.

THE PLEASURE OF THE TREASURE

So, yes, get ready to roll up your sleeves if you mean business in fulfilling your heart's desire. Commitment is a lifelong discipline of giving away all that you have for the sake of one awe-inspiring goal. This is the true foundation of achievement—a near obsession with converting potential into reality. But I don't want to oversell the idea of work and drudgery. That would be missing a very significant point about this matter of commitment.

When we chase our greatest goals, we come fully to life. Our eyes light up, and we begin to look a little bit more like the way God wants us to be. I believe God wanted me to go back and play my senior year of college football because I did it with a mind-set of glorifying him through the experience. I have already seen how God used that year in so many of his own ways.

Jesus gave two simple but wonderful parables that get the right idea across:

> Again, the kingdom of heaven is like treasure hidden in a field, which a man
> found and hid; and for joy over it he goes and sells all that he has and buys
> that field.

Again, the kingdom of heaven is like a merchant seeking beautiful pearls, who, when he had found one pearl of great price, went and sold all that he had and bought it. (Matthew 13:44–46)

Notice that in the first parable, a field laborer comes across a buried treasure. During the time in history when Jesus told this story, there were legends—if you will, the ancient version of urban myths—floating around about people unearthing old fortunes buried in the ground, where they had been hidden for safekeeping long ago. In an era of poverty, that would have been the ultimate fantasy; such a discovery would have been like hitting a first-century lottery.

Presumably this character reburies the treasure he has found. Then he goes home, gathers up everything he owns, and takes them to the pawnshop to turn them into cash. He takes the cash and buys the field where the treasure is buried so he will be the owner of the wonderful treasure he has discovered.

In the other story, one that is even simpler, a man is window-shopping when he spots the ultimate pearl, the "pearl of great price." His heart melts on the spot. Suddenly his entire universe comes down to this one item, and nothing else matters. He does just what the first fellow did—he trades in all he has just for the privilege of making this pearl his own.

In one story the wonderful thing was buried, and no one else in the world knew about it. In the other parable the treasure was, perhaps, sitting in a store or in someone else's possession. So the treasure, then, could be anything. It could be something buried deep within you—an idea that no one else has, a vision for art or literature or a new kind of business. Or it could be something other people see every day. But for you, it's the reason God put you here.

There are two points. One is that once the *wonderful thing* is identified, then total commitment is the only appropriate response. You are never going to be happy until you make that goal your own. But the other point is that it is a *joyful thing*. These two men gave away all they had, but I bet you didn't picture them moaning or whimpering, did you? They had just made the most important discoveries of their lives. They were ecstatic!

When we talk about the sacrifice of the great pianist, artist, writer, or athlete, we need to keep in mind that they are pursuing their own pearl of great price, their buried treasure. Talk to serious dream chasers, and they will tell you they wouldn't take anything for those hours of practice and perfection. Yes, they are totally committed, but it is not drudgery at all. It is a commitment that makes their eyes shine.

We are going to say a little more about the work required, but I don't want to give you the impression that pursuing your goal is joyless labor. Far from it—as a matter of fact, the best way to live a life of joyless labor is to turn away from your dream. God made you to go after some particular goal, and you will feel fully alive once you start chasing it. Someone else's drudgery becomes your personal slice of heaven. It is a commitment of joy and hope.

There are three components to powerful commitment. If you have a dream and want to achieve it someday, you must:

- want it more
- want it longer
- want it exclusively

Let's examine each of these three essentials.

WANTING IT MORE

We can all agree that we live in an age of wonders. In some ways that means our kids grow up with wider horizons. Nothing seems impossible in a world like this one.

On the other hand something has been lost. We have all become very comfortable, and that can have a chilling effect on the desire that is necessary for high achievement. Let me give you an example of what I am talking about.

President Larry Carter of Great Lakes Christian College has described what it was like to play Little League baseball when he was growing up. He says that when he was a youngster, there would be an annual cookout at the beginning of every new season. The coach would feed everybody burgers and dogs, then sit them down and have a pep talk. He would ask, "How many of you have ever dreamed of making it to the big league someday?"

Every single boy would immediately thrust a hand into the air, and you could see the glow in each boy's eyes. These boys spent leisurely hours collecting baseball cards and shared daydreams of appearing on a card one day themselves. They spent hours in the backyard playing catch and visualizing themselves in Yankee Stadium or Fenway Park.

The coach would then say, "Well, if you guys are going to make your dreams come true, it starts right here and right now." With that, the kids would start practicing with passion. Larry and his teammates were powerfully motivated to work hard. Their team went undefeated for several consecutive seasons.

Larry grew up and in his spare time became a coach himself. He couldn't wait to duplicate what his coaches had taught him about motivation when he was younger. He had a cookout, invited the kids, and asked the big question: "How many of you dream of growing up and playing in the majors?"

But this time, not a single hand went into the air! No young eyes glowed; as a matter of fact, the looks in them were dubious.

Larry Carter said that he was haunted by the change that had come over young people in twenty-five years.

I think about this and wonder if it is really a question of commitment. I believe these modern kids would have said they would *like* to play in the majors—if they didn't get a thrill from the game, they wouldn't have signed up for Little League, right? But Larry's generation grew up outdoors, playing ball in backyards and empty lots.

You see, there weren't so many *other things* to do. Have you ever noticed what luxuries modern kids have available to them? Baseball cards probably seem boring—it is all about technology now. These kids have gaming consoles, hundreds of channels of television, computers, portable music players with thousands of songs, and their own cell phones.

Drive around a few neighborhoods during the summer and tell me how many kids you see riding their bikes or playing catch outdoors. I think if you were to sit some of these kids down and ask, "Why *don't* you dream of playing in the majors?" perhaps they'd say, "Are you kidding? Too much work!"

I'm not knocking our kids or the way we raise them, though most of them could stand a little fresh air. But isn't this change true of all of us? Don't the luxuries of life water down our resolve to achieve something special? In the story that opened this chapter, Sylvester Stallone didn't have to walk away from comfort and luxury to achieve his goal; he had none. But he was *focused*. He believed in himself, and he wanted to show he could do something special, all the more since he had walked a tough road. History teaches us that the furnace of life refines the stuff that creates high achievers.

It is important, therefore, for us to think about distractions. How much do we really want this thing? Are we willing to give up a few TV shows to work toward whatever the goal may be? Would we settle for a simpler, less luxurious lifestyle in order to begin accumulating the financial resources we will need for the pursuit?

It's amazing how often Jesus spoke about this simple principle. For example, he used the word picture of a man setting out to build a tower—a nice metaphor for a dream or an impressive goal:

> For which of you, intending to build a tower, does not sit down first and count the cost, whether he has enough to finish it—lest, after he has laid the foundation, and is not able to finish, all who see it begin to mock him, saying, "This man began to build and was not able to finish." (Luke 14:28–30)

As a carpenter, Jesus would have known that if you measure twice, you will only need to cut once. Consider what you are up against. In the case of our goals, the opposition is usually not from without but from within. Today's tower builder can probably find the funding. What it really comes down to is, does he or she want it enough?

WANTING IT LONGER

"You have to want it more," the principle we have just discussed, is something of a coaching cliché. I heard it for years, and if you have spent much time around athletes, I bet you have heard it too. But through my fitness coaching career, my philosophy on that point evolved. Wanting it more is a good start, but you had better want it longer too.

When I got into the strength-and-conditioning field at the college level, the whole idea of strength coaching as a systematic discipline was just coming together. It was a good fit for me because I had retained my passion for strength training and staying in shape even after my playing career seemed to be over. I also tend to be logical and systematic, as well as aggressive, motivational, and hands-on. Therefore, I was seemingly made for directing a strength program for college athletes or anyone else for that matter.

In learning the ropes for my line of work, here is what I discovered. My critical season was the fans' off-season. That is, by the time a team suited up to play its first game, the bulk of my work was done. The strength and conditioning of a player's body is a year-round process, but it is during the spring and summer in particular that the players really hit the weight room. This is the time when the most successful players are focused and motivated. They come in, work through the circuit to exercise every muscle group, and set goals for their achievements by the end of summer when fall practice begins in earnest.

This is where wanting-it-longer comes into play. All of these kids are motivated when the stands are full, the band is playing, and the opponent is standing on the other sideline. But you won't come out on top in November if you didn't take care of business in July. When the fourth quarter of the game comes and the score is tied, the team in the best condition will win the game in the trenches (at the lines of scrimmage). At that moment wanting it more only makes a difference if the team has wanted it longer because conditioning is the fruit of effort multiplied by time.

We would challenge those athletes to get up early, go run some stadiums, and do even more than was required of them. We would tell them, "When you're tempted to roll over in bed and sleep late in the morning, just know that your rival isn't sleeping late. He's up working on his body, perfecting his skills because he wants to line up against you and whip you this season. He's living for that moment. If you want to come out on top, the battle is won right now."

I am motivated by being told I can't do something. When I was twelve, my father lost his temper and told me I was a runt and that was all I'd ever be. I was crushed and hurting inside when I went to bed that night, and I wished with all that was in me that I would wake up as a larger and more powerful individual. The next morning I was still a runt, but I resolved that if there was anything in my power I could do to change that, I was going to make it happen.

At the age of fifteen I was five foot three and weighed 104 pounds. By the time I earned a starting position on the first state championship football team at Permian High School, I was eight inches taller and forty-four pounds heavier. I had increased my weight by nearly 50 percent, and none of it was fat.

But I wasn't going to be satisfied until I heard my dad acknowledge that I was no longer a runt. For ten years that was my goal for every waking moment. It was the thing that drove me beyond fatigue, as misguided a goal as that was. I was twenty-two when Dad finally conceded the point, and I can tell you today exactly where I was standing and what I was wearing when he said these words: "You finally made the man I always wanted you to be."

The interesting thing is that I kept wanting it. After playing college football for three years, I found myself out in the job world still working to avoid being a runt. I had paid too high a price to let my strength and conditioning deteriorate just because I wasn't putting on a helmet and pads. I made a commitment at twelve, picked up speed, and crossed the finish line ten years later—but you could say I kept on running. I was committed.

Or to put it more accurately, I wanted it longer.

The goals we seek have to do with changing our destiny in some way—usually altering something exterior. You may want to start a consulting firm, sing in concerts, or become a foreign missionary. Whatever your goal might be, you are going to find that what changed most is not in the world outside you but in the world inside you. My pursuit was the simple avoidance of "runthood," but it became something deeper as I grew and matured. God connected my misguided goal with his perfect will—a beautiful thing that he often does for us.

Wanting it more plus wanting it longer adds up to a lifelong process of changing who you are. At the time we think it is about the destination; in the end it is probably more about the journey.

Fleeting wishes are no more than distractions; genuine dreams, pursued seriously and enduringly, utterly transform who we are.

WANTING IT EXCLUSIVELY

We've mentioned music a couple of times in this chapter. Let's discuss that field again. Luciano Pavarotti was an Italian tenor who died in 2007. He may have been the most successful opera singer of his time. How he developed his talent is a classic example of commitment.

Luciano's father, a baker by trade, loved music and introduced his son to it. But Luciano did the hard work, practicing and training with a professional tenor for years in order to develop his voice while also taking classes at a teacher's college. Upon graduation Luciano was faced with a decision. Should he be a teacher or a singer? Or should he consider doing both? His father wisely advised him that to try to sing and teach at the same time would be like trying to sit in two chairs; there would always be the risk of falling between the two. He needed to make a choice.

Luciano chose to sing. His first professional appearance came after seven years of study, frustration, and dedication, then the Metropolitan Opera seven long years after that. Luciano had made a life choice, but his commitment to that choice was the key to his success.[1]

Two roads diverge in the woods. Which one will you choose? Too many people try to go in more than one direction. Recently we have seen the proliferation of these wonderful little gadgets called GPS (Global Positioning System) navigators. The device is installed on the dashboard of your car, and it directs you anywhere you want to go. A nice voice even tells you exactly when to turn and how much farther you need to drive. But the device will only select one route at a time and take you to one destination at a time.

If you are serious about your dream, your mind needs to work in exactly the same way. You need a mental GPS that understands your destination and calculates the best route to get you there. Think of God as the voice that speaks to you and guides you along the way, over the bumps in the road, past the traffic jams and construction sites, and toward the place where your heart is set on arriving.

By the way, I often saw athletes who had to make a tough decision. In high school they had excelled in multiple sports. In football they may have played on both sides of the ball. But as recruits for a major college football program, it usually made sense for them to focus on one sport and within that sport, one position. There is the occasional Bo Jackson or Deion Sanders who can play two major sports without sacrificing in either, but those are the exceptions rather than the rule.

We might tell a player, "I know how much you love basketball, but football provides your best future, and that means building and maintaining a football body twelve months per year." We would also say, "As great a time as you had playing quarterback in high school, your best future is at free safety. We don't want you dividing your learning time between two positions."

This was a demanding adjustment for students who played sports for the joy of it. Sometimes (particularly as hotshot recruits), they would balk at the wise counsel of experienced coaches. They might say, "I will only entertain scholarship offers from schools that let me play quarterback" (or some other position). You could even say a player's *dream* was to play quarterback rather than free safety.

Should the coaches tinker with someone's dream? It depends on how grounded in wisdom the dream is. Sometimes God uses other people to help us discover what our hearts really yearn for.

University of Georgia football coach Mark Richt grew up in South Florida with a passion for baseball. At the high school level a smart coach told him that football could get him a college scholarship while baseball probably wouldn't. Richt then had to decide whether his real dream was to play baseball or whether it was to have a college education. He opted for the latter and ended up making football a career—again, it was smart to write his dream onto his heart in pencil. The athletic passion was the true center, not baseball.

On the other hand, some write in ink, and who can say they are wrong? I know a young man who was asked to name his dream job in third grade. I think we can agree that most eight-year-olds have yet to get a handle on what they are supposed to do in life—I know some forty-year-olds who haven't figured it out yet. At any rate, each third grader in this particular class was asked by the teacher to place numbers on a card, from one to three, and write down their top three choices for jobs when they entered the working world.

When the kids passed their cards to the front of the class, the teacher began reading the responses—teaching, the law, the medical profession, and so forth. She paused when she came to one particular card. "Someone wants to be a professional basketball player," she said. "And whoever did this listed it not only as first choice but as second and third as well."

The teacher briefly explained to the class why this was an unrealistic job choice. She said that very few young men ever make it to the National Basketball Association—many play while in high school, far fewer make it to the collegiate level, and then only one in hundreds of thousands makes it all the way to the NBA. The teacher wanted to know who had turned in that card.

A young man raised his hand. The teacher asked him why he didn't at least provide two choices, and he replied, "Because I'm going to play in the NBA. For me there are no other choices."

Wise counsel might have prevailed upon him to broaden his horizons, but he happened to have the right dream. He is LeBron James of the Cleveland Cavaliers—top NBA draft choice out of *high school*, Rookie of the Year, 2008–2009 NBA Most Valuable Player.

He beat the odds, and in his case I'm glad he stuck to his dream, just as Sylvester Stallone did.

But his success is the result of a God-given gift, in addition to wanting it more, wanting it longer, and particularly wanting it exclusively. For him, there were no other choices.

How about for you?

THE MOMENT OF DECISION

There comes a defining moment when you must decide which road to choose. It is time to come to terms with what is inside you: Is that thing a wish, or is it a genuine dream? Have you been indulging in harmless fantasy, or are you hearing an internal call for the adventure of a lifetime?

Again Jesus shows us what this idea is all about. One day, as the Gospels tell us, a young man approached him with great excitement. In Mark 10:17 we are told that he came running up to Jesus and knelt down. He was clearly captivated by the amazing ideas he had heard from this new teacher in Galilee, this man who seemed to know so much about God.

He asked Jesus what he could do to gain eternal life.

Jesus sized him up. It was clear from the young man's appearance that he was a person of wealth and privilege. He would have stood out like a sore thumb among the peasants who surrounded Jesus.

Jesus engaged the questioner in a dialogue as he often did. He began by saying, "You know the commandments." And he started reciting them—don't murder, don't commit adultery . . .

Naturally this idea didn't satisfy the rich young man. He knew Jesus had much more to say on the theme than that! He said dismissively, "I've obeyed all those commandments since I was very young."

The Bible tells us Jesus looked at him and felt love for him. In my opinion, this wasn't because he believed this fellow had really managed to keep all of the Ten Commandments from childhood but because he saw just how little this young man knew himself.

Jesus told him to sell all that he had since he would have riches in heaven. Then he said, "Take up the cross, and follow Me" (Mark 10:21). The first task would be very difficult for a person immersed in riches; the second would be demanding for anyone on this planet since the cross was not a religious symbol, as it is today, but a description of torturous execution for the lowest criminals.

What Jesus said hit that man right between the eyes. The rich young man turned around and walked away.

The point of this story isn't that we all need to sell our possessions if we want to follow Jesus any more than it is that we need to apply for criminal execution. What it is about is the moment of decision. Jesus was saying, "Are you interested in a passing fad, or are you really ready to walk this road? These men with me have left their possessions behind; many of them will, in fact, die for me and for my name's sake. They have made a choice."

Let me reaffirm that it is a choice of joy, not of ongoing pain. Jesus was speaking to one particular man who needed to know the seriousness of the question he was asking. Yes, there is talk in the Bible of our taking up our crosses, but Jesus also said he came to give us abundant life; he said the kingdom of God is buried treasure. I have followed Jesus now for many years, and I can tell you that it is a life of wonderful fulfillment and purpose.

But I wouldn't tell anyone to take up Jesus the way they would take up collecting stamps or coins. The life of faith is serious business, and there needs to be a brutally honest time of cost counting up front. Following Jesus is about a radical life change, and the rich young man was confronted by the realization that he really didn't want that.

You will need to answer the same question. Are you ready to follow the path that you believe God is calling you to walk? Are you ready to commit yourself?

I'll tell you what I have told a lot of young athletes in the weight room. This is not going to be easy. There will be days when you feel every impulse to take the path of least resistance. You are going to have to want it more than the other guy. You are going to have to want it longer. And you are going to have to walk away from some other things you might enjoy doing—choices your friends make, choices you would make if you didn't have greater goals in mind.

A good gardener prunes a tree or a vine. He or she cuts away the extra sprouts that divert the life-giving fluids from the portion that bears fruit. Pruning is painful, but it is necessary.

When you have done these things—put in the work, put in the time, and put away the distractions—you are going to experience a wonderful, clarifying focus in your life. You are going to have more energy and purpose because you know exactly where you are going. And even though you won't realize it—because your eyes will be focused ahead of you, on your new horizon—you will be changing, growing, improving, and becoming the best version of you that is possible. As one great athlete said, "I choose to suffer in this moment so that I can be a champion for the rest of my life."

Win the small victory now, follow this path, and you will be a champion who wins the big victory. Defeat the bear, and later you will defeat Goliath.

Your goal will grow and change as much as you will. But you will accomplish other things you never even intended. You will be effective and successful at other parts of life simply because you gained wisdom from this part of it. You will have a powerful influence over other people because most are not goal-driven. They wander aimlessly until they see someone who seems to know where he is going, and they fall into line behind that person. You will become a role model.

Finally, you will have the joy of being precisely where your destiny intended you to be. If you happen to be a follower of Christ, you will know that you are carrying out a plan for which you were lovingly designed at the foundation of time.

For that reason you are going to have optimal joy and optimal satisfaction. And you will leave the world a better place than you found it. Isn't that worth the cost of commitment?

7
····

Team: Know Who You Play For

The year was 1984, and Michael Jordan was one month into his rookie year as a basketball player for the Chicago Bulls. *Sports Illustrated* magazine featured him on its cover with the title "A Star Is Born." Even at road games fans of the other teams would chant the newcomer's name as Air Jordan made spectacular slam dunks in pregame warm-ups.

Jealousy began to rear its ugly head. When Jordan was voted to start on the All-Star team as a rookie, some of the veteran players refused to pass him the ball. Michael Jordan had learned his first discouraging lesson in team dynamics.

Eventually the Chicago Bulls became the most dominant force in the league. But that took a number of years. Jordan was already averaging a staggering twenty-eight points per game as a rookie, and his defensive game was nearly as impressive. During seven great years of individual play, Jordan averaged as many as thirty-five points per game. But somehow Chicago's total team performance added up to less than the sum of its parts. The team's coach, Phil Jackson, said,

Back in the late eighties, I used to remind Michael Jordan that, as many great scoring games as he had, he still sometimes ended up coming out on the losing end, because he would try to beat the other team by himself. Even though he could pull it off occasionally, we weren't going to win consistently until the other players on our team started helping us.[1]

The turning point came in the final 1991 playoff game against the Los Angeles Lakers. The Lakers were keying in on Jordan, the obvious strategy for beating Chicago in those days. Coach Jackson insisted that his star let the defenders collapse in on him and then get the ball out to teammate John Paxson on the perimeter.

Jordan had to suppress every athletic instinct he had and begin making simple passes. Eventually Paxson made the winning shot to establish the Bulls's first of three consecutive championships, the famous three-peat. That was Jordan's second lesson in team dynamics.

From there, his team began to hit on all cylinders, becoming unstoppable simply because they committed themselves to functioning in unity. Players knew their roles and stuck to them. One result was that a second superstar, Scottie Pippen, emerged; the biggest results, however, were seen in the win column and the trophy case.

Phil Jackson reflected that the time came when he hardly needed to coach. The team instinct was so powerful and the players knew each other's moves so well that they created their own winning strategies in the process. Jackson has said that "creating any kind of team is a spiritual act. People have to surrender their own egos, so that the end result is bigger than the sum of its parts."[2]

When Jordan emerged from retirement to play with the Washington Wizards in 2001, he found, during preseason scrimmages, that his new teammates expected him to carry them. They would pass him the ball and then stop to see what he would do. So Jordan established a new policy for the preseason: he imposed a no-shoot rule on himself. Even with the scrimmage on the line, he would not take the shot. Thus he forced his new teammates to learn the lesson the Chicago Bulls had learned. Michael Jordan, basketball's greatest individual talent, was now teaching the doctrine of teamwork.

It's pretty obvious where I'm going with this. Team strategy is for everyone, not just athletes. But you might beg to differ when it comes to chasing your dream. You might say, for example, that while there is no *I* in *TEAM*, there are two of them in *VISION*. After all, prophets don't work by committee, do they? Artists don't produce paintings or symphonies by taking votes. If the ark had been constructed by a committee, would it have ever floated?

You could say these things, and you would have a point. In general, dreams and visions come to us as individuals. And certain achievements must be done solo—including a beautiful slam dunk by Michael Jordan. But who got Jordan in position to take the shot?

Look into your own private heart to find your dream. Depend on what God is telling you to know what direction you should follow. No one can discover that but you. But whatever great goal you pursue, unless you live on a deserted island, you will be required to depend on others. That is the difference between a star and a champion.

Let's examine the team dynamic and explore how you can establish it as a power base in your quest for excellence.

ALL FOR ONE AND ONE FOR ALL

As Jesus prepared to give his life for us, one of his final earthly actions was to teach his disciples to function as a team. You might remember how the Twelve bickered along the road to Jerusalem. Even as their teacher warned them what event lay ahead, they argued about which of them was the greatest. Even their mothers got into the act, advocating their own sons for the best positions when Christ came into his kingdom.

In the Upper Room at that final meal together, Jesus taught a different mind-set. Not only did he know the pain he would soon experience, but he knew which of his beloved friends would betray him. Yet as the time approached for him to sacrifice his body, his only concern was that they learn to function as one unit. Listen to John's description:

> Jesus, knowing that the Father had given all things into His hands, and that
> He had come from God and was going to God, rose from supper and laid

aside His garments, took a towel and girded Himself. After that, He poured water into a basin and began to wash the disciples' feet, and to wipe them with the towel with which He was girded. (John 13:3–5)

Michael Jordan only thought he could carry a team on his back. If ever anyone lived who had the right to that belief, it was Jesus. As verse 3 tells us, he knew that God "had given all things into His hands," that he "had come from God and was going to God." He would take the sins of the world upon his shoulders. Yet he created a living picture that no one in the room would ever forget. He began to wash everyone's feet. In that part of the world, no act could be considered lower or dirtier. The religious system valued absolute cleanliness and purity above anything else. The idea of a group's master stooping to do something like this was shocking.

Peter objected to the gesture and even tried to forbid it. But Jesus told him that he must allow himself to be served, or he would not be part of the group. Afterward Jesus said, "If I then, your Lord and Teacher, have washed your feet, you also ought to wash one another's feet. For I have given you an example, that you should do as I have done to you" (vv. 14–15).

Jesus understood that after he was gone, these proud men, bonded only by their love for him, must be bonded by their love for one another. They must stop competing and start cooperating, for they would be expected to achieve the impossible. As Jesus reached them, they must reach the entire world. Without radical unity they would never pass the city limits.

Jesus went on to talk to the disciples about the relationships they must have with one another. He said, "A new commandment I give to you, that you love one another, even as I have loved you, that you also love one another. By this all men will know that you are My disciples, if you have love for one another" (vv. 34–35 NASB).

There is a special kind of relationship among members of a group when they are bonded in unity for a common purpose. I have seen it many times in athletic contexts, and any veteran of the military service can tell you about it too. It is possible to love your team or your squad or your department or your class enough to be ready to give yourself sacrificially for its members. It is an all-for-one-and-one-for-all mentality. And when it sets in, there is no limit to what a group of ordinary individuals can accomplish. The whole becomes greater than the sum of its parts.

WHO ARE YOU PLAYING FOR?

Have you ever been part of a dysfunctional organization? It's very frustrating.

Many businesses today are dysfunctional. Due to the economic pressures we see in the workplace, the tension is ratcheted up. People look out for themselves and try to undermine their peers. Some people are experts at shifting responsibility to someone else rather than volunteering to do extra. True camaraderie is replaced by superficial office politics. In time it will drag down any organization.

In sports you see some teams that have incredible chemistry and others that self-destruct. Good coaches set the tone, but sometimes there are situations in which even the coaches can't turn around people's attitudes. Even one player with a poisonous attitude can be a cancer to the entire organization—the proverbial bad apple that spoils the barrel. But it doesn't have to be that way.

When I speak to athletes today, I talk about my experiences as a young player and coach in the late fifties, the sixties, and the seventies, and even as an ordinary fan.

My 2007 senior year, coming after decades of ordinary life lessons, brought me to some profound conclusions about the nature of a team. I decided there is a remarkable power, an almost supernatural bond between human beings when a team is functioning correctly. It is refined in the hot furnace of common preparation and sacrifice. It begins when players cross a certain decisive point: they knock down the walls of individuality and choose to give themselves to the common purpose. They stop playing for themselves and begin playing for each other, and it takes their game to a whole new level.

I will never forget the day during that 2007 season I figured this out. We were playing conference rival East Texas Baptist University. That was a tough contest for us because the opposing team had a personnel advantage—it had more talent, more depth. Even so, we had taken a 21–7 lead in the first quarter, and things were looking good. Then a series of questionable play calls deep in our own territory shortened the field for our opponent. The result was three easy touchdowns for ETBU. At halftime we had fallen behind by seven points.

In the locker room our head coach was furious. He raised his voice and commanded the trainers, assistant coaches, and medical personnel to get out of the room. Then he accused us, his team, of quitting on him in the second quarter. He could see it in our eyes and on our faces, he shouted, and he couldn't stand quitters. Then he actually walked out on us. He said, "You're on your own now," slammed the door behind him, and stormed away.

Sitting there in the silence of that locker room, I realized what a team is all about. A coach can walk away, but a team remains intact. *We play for each other*. We are the guys in the trenches, taking the physical beatings that football dishes out. We are the ones who work throughout the year for those eleven or twelve sixty-minute periods of regulation. We are the ones who suffer the painful knee injuries, the multiple bruises, and the long-term-injury gifts that keep giving long after we are finished playing. Sometimes we are carried out on stretchers, having given our very best and paid the price. Sometimes we hear the boos of fans who only sit, watch, and eat their popcorn; these folks, like the coach, can walk out on us if it appears we are going to lose. Anyone can quit—anyone but the guys wearing the numbers.

We will never quit on each other.

That, in a nutshell, is what makes us a team.

Have you ever seen a game in which the players on the field looked over to the bench and found it empty? Ever seen a group of players say, "Hey, we're out of here; we've got better things to do"? I had never seen a coach quit on his team, but when it happened, it became a moment of crystallization in my understanding.

As soon as the door slammed, I leaped to my feet. Maybe the coach knew all along what I was going to do. Who knows? "Listen to me," I shouted. "Nobody in here has quit—not a one of you! The only one who did just left the room. But look around you now. There is no one here but us. Nobody but the people we play for: each other. Everywhere we go and in everything we do, we represent this university. But when we step out on that field of play, we play for each other. And if the fans quit and the coaches quit, that's okay, but we won't quit on each other."

I went on to say how important it was to avoid pointing the finger. We win as a team, we lose as a team, and the one mistake we can't afford is to break rank. It was time to link arms, get back out on the field, and show what we were made of.

We played our hearts out in the second half. We couldn't salvage the victory, but I think we learned something that will stay in all of our hearts for the rest of our lives: as long as we hold together as a team, we have a victory that no one can take away. As for the game itself, I like to win; who doesn't? I was prepared to sacrifice my body, take the blows, and do what was required to come out on top in the score. But the victory of team unity is sweeter and more enduring. Like a few of the bumps and bruises, team identity is a gift that keeps giving as you go through life.

That's what I learned. Now let's talk about how you can apply it. What are the teams that will become your power base as you chase your dreams? We all function in various kinds of groups and organizations, but there are three that will make the biggest difference in your future.

FIRST TEAM

Your first team is always going to be the family unit. It is impossible to have a positive career life on top of a negative family life. It's simply the way God made us and the way we structure society. We call it the *nuclear* family because it is at the very center of our world as the nucleus is the center of the atom.

God established the family when he first created us. He said, "It is not good that man should be alone" (Genesis 2:18). Later God added, "Therefore a man shall leave his father and mother and be joined to his wife, and they shall become one flesh" (v. 24). The family is, therefore, our most ancient institution and the foundation of society. It is your first team and the one you are playing for every day in all that you do.

As the family goes, so goes the culture. Maintaining a family means honoring traditional marriage and parenthood. In recent days, of course, we have begun to play fast and loose with the definition and importance of family. That accounts for so many of the problems we see during our nation's moral decline. Many studies show that the institution of marriage is in trouble. Divorce statistics within the church match those outside of it, and children are suffering from the dissolution of their parents' marriages.

The psalmist described children as "arrows in the hand of a warrior" (Psalm 127:4). Think about that metaphor. The bow is a long-distance weapon. We aim our children toward the right values and fire them into the future, where they will have an impact far beyond our years. Our children are dreams and visions in themselves, opportunities to invest in our afterlife and to leave the world better than we found it.

But what if we neglect our spouses and our children because we are too focused on our work? It is clear enough that many driven leaders do this today. Somehow we come to believe that we are defined by our jobs and our goals rather than by the identity God has given us. Instead of being arrows fired into the future, children become collateral damage.

Not that we are likely to be successful anyway if there is a faulty foundation at home. A loving family strengthens us for the great tasks of life. We need to share our dreams with family members and include them in every way possible, making them partners in the greater goals we pursue. Have you ever had a family meeting simply to talk about your long-range vision and ask family members for their prayers and assistance? Does your spouse function as your most important advisor?

Not everyone, of course, is married. Paul actually explained in 1 Corinthians 7 that remaining unmarried can be an advantage in certain cases. The single person can have a flexible life with lower expenses. He or she can be on the move whenever needed. Unmarried people are doing great things, for instance, in overseas missions these days. But even singles need family. In their case our second form of team comes into play.

THE SUPPORT TEAM

One of the most common mistakes made by failed leaders today is allowing themselves to be above accountability. With no one to pray for them and to provide "tough love" where necessary, they are far more likely to fall into temptation. Without wise counsel, these people lack the crucial added perspective in decision making. Singles have the extra need for these relationships when spouses and children are not present. A small group of peers, often found in church fellowship, can become a family in itself.

The Quakers have an interesting tradition in this regard. When a leader has a momentous decision to make, he or she will call on a "clearness committee" of about a dozen close friends. They won't give advice; instead, they will spend three hours asking challenging questions that help the person objectively clarify the wisest decision.

In the early Methodist movement John Wesley did something similar. The practice was called "watching over one another in love." People wanting to enter spiritual fellowship with these Christians would be asked questions to determine whether or not they were ready to live in mutual accountability. Here are some sample questions:

- Do you desire to be told of your faults?
- Consider—do you desire that we should tell you whatsoever we think, whatsoever we fear, whatsoever we hear concerning you?
- Do you desire that in doing this we should come as close as possible, that we should cut to the quick, and search your heart to the bottom?
- Is it your desire and design to be on this and all other occasions entirely open, so as to speak everything that is in your heart, without exception, without disguise, and without reserve?[3]

The Bible teaches us to confess our sins to each other (James 5:16). It also teaches that we should gently help each other toward the right decisions in life. But that is not always easy for even the most disciplined among us. According to a 2005 survey by Georgetown University's Center for Applied Research on the Apostolate, only 2 percent of Catholics say they go regularly to the confessional sessions that are part of their church tradition.[4]

Even those of us with wonderful marriage partners need someone outside the family circle to help us. We all need both a Paul and a Timothy—that is, an older mentor to counsel us and a younger friend to counsel.

We can only have so many close friends. In this age of Facebook and blogging, we have more acquaintances than ever but fewer true friends. Who could you call in the middle of the night if you had a crisis? Who could you call on to pray for you if you were struggling with sexual temptation? And who is actually capable of reining you in when necessary? We grow so busy, so focused on achievement, that we forget just how critical it is that we have help.

An accountability group can be as small as one other close person as long as you are meeting regularly and sharing honestly. More typically, a small Bible study or prayer group—no larger than a dozen people—performs this function. The important thing is that you allow God to speak into your life through trusted friends and that you are speaking into the lives of others.

That group, by the way, should not be the same as our third category. It should be separate from your life pursuit so that everyone can be fully objective.

THE DREAM TEAM

As the name implies, your dream team is the group of people with whom you go after your great goal. In many cases this is a group of coworkers. As we know, however, some office groups can be closer to nightmares than dreams.

Then again, your job may not be the same as your dream. You could dream of starting your own company in the same business, or you could have a vision that is totally different. For example, you could be a tax accountant who wants to start an Internet retail business. In that case maybe you have a friend who is part of the team you would like to build to launch that Web site. Perhaps you are already working in your spare time to build good business relationships—an Internet service provider, a wholesaler, whatever.

Ask God to direct you to people who share your vision. This, of course, will end up being the team of people to whom you entrust your life purpose if you're pursuing a big dream. They could help push it across the finish line, or they could sabotage the whole endeavor. For that reason you want to assemble that group deliberately and with plenty of prayer, taking care that you know these people very well. Some people go into business with old friends. There are advantages to that, of course, but bumps in the road have put premature ends to many good friendships.

Paul's New Testament travels make a good case study of a dream team. We know of several significant partnerships he had—with Luke, with John Mark, with Silas, and with Barnabas, for example. Each one of these seemed to provide some different dynamic to the vision Paul had for reaching the Mediterranean world with the gospel. Barnabas was Paul's mentor in many ways, an encourager who was always quietly working in the background. His personality was a near-perfect complement to that of Paul, who could be more aggressive and was also more of a visionary leader.

God used Paul's team relationships in a number of interesting ways. For example, Paul and Barnabas clashed bitterly over whether to take John Mark on a trip (Acts 15:39). Paul argued that the younger missionary had failed an earlier test, giving up and going home. He felt that John Mark had already had his chance while Barnabas held out for grace and a fresh opportunity. The two groups could not agree and went in different directions, Paul with Silas and Barnabas with John Mark. As a result the missionary work was doubled. As for Luke, God used him to observe and record all the events so that the world could be blessed with them. Timothy became the recipient of instructional letters from Paul—letters that have instructed the rest of us for twenty centuries. Paul's team served him in all the ways he had hoped but in many ways he never could have dreamed.

God will do that for your team too. In other words, even during difficult times and disagreements, he will work in ways you may never anticipate. Build your team carefully, looking for various skills and profiles. The important thing is that everyone shares the same long-range goal.

Those, then, are three key teams to maintain. Now, in terms of your team goals, how should you be organized? Let's talk about three rules for play.

PLAY BY POSITION

First, we know from football that it won't do to have a skinny wide receiver play linebacker. In any organized sport we figure out how to use our personnel based on their natural skills. I know how obvious that sounds, but let's think about how it applies in the work world. In the New Testament we read:

> For as we have many members in one body, but all the members do not have the same function, so we, being many, are one body in Christ, and individually members of one another. Having then gifts differing according to the grace that is given to us, let us use them. (Romans 12:4–6)

We all know everyone has a different skill set, but have you ever noticed how often we ignore that simple truth? In churches, ministries, and organizations of every kind, we tend to plug available people into available spots. I know that in churches, one of the key underlying causes of friction is the misuse of spiritual gifts. When we are all doing what we do best, things just seem to click.

One reason we go wrong is we establish pecking orders. Because we characterize one job as being more important than another, people go after jobs for status reasons rather than trying to do the things God made them to do. We ordain people based on traits such as social prominence rather than determining which gifts are needed and who has those gifts.

The church was still in its infancy when factions began forming. Some said they were in the Paul camp; others supported a teacher named Apollos. Paul wrote:

> Who then is Paul, and who is Apollos, but ministers through whom you believed, as the Lord gave to each one? I planted, Apollos watered, but God gave the increase. So then neither he who plants is anything, nor he who waters, but God who gives the increase. Now he who plants and he who waters are one, and each one will receive his own reward according to his own labor. For we are God's fellow workers; you are God's field, you are God's building. (1 Corinthians 3:5–9)

"No one is superior," Paul was saying. "We just have different responsibilities." When we play by position and forget who gets the credit or why, God's Spirit is liberated, and good things begin to happen.

It is the same in the business world. Office politics begin to set in, and we get tangled up in hierarchies and other issues instead of putting people where they can get the most done and then getting to work. When you work in a group—any group—do you do a careful study of personality types and gift sets? There are many ways to assess traits and gifts. Human resources directors can help you with inventories and tests that measure people's skill orientations. There are also good tests that suggest what a person's spiritual gifts might be.

The Greeks said, "Know thyself." What is your best position? Think of it this way. Earlier in the book we talked about the idea of the sweet spot. A tennis racquet has one. Hit the ball in that spot, and you have the most control over where it goes and how fast. Baseball bats have sweet spots that drive the ball farther. People have sweet spots that cause them to work with extra joy and success when the task and the spot come together.

We do tend to gravitate toward the tasks with which we feel the most comfortable, but for various reasons we can end up in jobs and positions unsuitable for us. Do you know yourself? For example, are you more comfortable teaching and motivating a group or working quietly in the background? Are you more comfortable with numbers or intangible concepts? Do you tend to see the forest best or the trees?

These are questions for which there aren't right or wrong answers—it is simply a matter of how God made you. Perhaps the single element that tells the most about you is your dream. If it is the right one—the enduring one—then God placed it in you, and you can be assured that he gave you the gifts and talents to go with it.

PLAY AS A UNIT

The most underrated word in the New Testament is *unity*. Each of the letters to the churches speaks of the unity that believers must have. When the devil wants to destroy our work, he targets our unity. He tries to come between us and turn us against each other.

It is almost shocking when we read what Jesus said on the subject during that final prayer for his friends in the Upper Room. He prayed to the Father about the kind of unity he wants us to have:

And the glory which You gave Me I have given them, that they may be one just as We are one: I in them, and You in Me; that they may be made perfect in one, and that the world may know that You have sent Me, and have loved them as You have loved Me. (John 17:22–23)

Did you catch that? He's talking about the unity within the Trinity, the very person of God! As the Father, Son, and Spirit work in perfect harmony with one another, so are we to do that very same thing. What an incredible thought: "that [we] may be made perfect in one." Yet it is absolutely consistent with what the Bible teaches: *We* are the representatives of the Father, the Son, and the Holy Spirit to those who do not believe, so we must measure up. *We* are the only Bible that some people will ever read. We would be terrified by these ideas if not for two things:

- God has promised his presence and his power wherever we go.
- God has given us each other—and together, we are the body of Christ.

Therefore, insofar as we are followers of Christ, we must learn to function as a well-oiled team. But these are universal principles too. They work for everybody. Any kind of team is stronger when its members have unity. Any group is greater than the sum of its parts when everyone learns his or her role.

We have to go to the animal kingdom for the best pictures of working together in perfect harmony. You may have heard about the remarkable range of the geese that migrate from Canada to the southern United States when cold weather comes. Scientists have been astounded by the fact that these fowl can travel thousands of miles in an organized fashion. It is clear that they could never make the journey as individual birds.

They travel in that familiar V formation that makes such a beautiful sight in the autumn sky. Fighter pilots, by the way, began taking their cue from the geese many years ago—it's just good aerodynamics, and it saves fuel. Each goose creates an upward air current for the one behind him. It is estimated that by flying in the V pattern, the flock gets 71 percent greater range than each would get in a solo flight.

The front goose, the point in the V, rotates that position with the others.

Obviously he faces the most wind resistance, and when he tires, he drops to the end of the line where he can rest in the best spot. One of the two geese behind him rotates into position. And the back geese do the honking. We can't be sure, but it may be that they are signaling that everyone is in position, and all is well.

What about when they are not fine? Old and sick birds fly in the center, where it is easiest, and if a bird becomes wounded or too ill to continue, two others escort it to the ground and stand guard, waiting until the sick bird can fly again.

The geese are God's example of how we should work together as a team. They accept the enormous challenge of flying thousands of miles in a short time and are then prepared to return in season. Together they get it done in a way that is systematic, efficient, and protective of every member. Think again about Michael Jordan and the Chicago Bulls. Having the best player in the league—probably in history—only made them a competitive team. Playing together as a fully committed unit made them a dynasty.

Think about the organizations you are a part of—your family, your church or small group, your business organization. How well do you communicate among yourselves? How do the members protect each other in times of weakness or struggle? How are tasks rotated or distributed for the most efficiency? We would all do well to create an ongoing report card, giving grades for these factors and others.

Let's pull together and play as a team!

PLAY FOR EACH OTHER

We have seen in Romans 12 how Paul said we are "members of one another." I like that phrase a lot. We aren't simply members of the same organization. We are members of one another. You can ignore someone who lives in the same neighborhood, goes to the same church, or maybe even lives in the same house. But if someone is a dues-paying official member of *you*—well, that's different.

Frankly, the only other situation being members of one another resembles is marriage. A husband and wife belong intimately to one another. Two people deeply in love live for one another through their marriage and do everything to meet each other's needs. But remember, in a way unity among believers *is* marriage: the church is described as the bride of Christ. So it is not surprising that we are to have a relationship that rivals the best of marriages. That is something to think about, isn't it?

The New Testament has a series of one-another statements. A quick concordance search shows the series of things that we do when we are members of one another: We are to be:

admonishing one another; bearing one another's burdens; bearing with one another in love; hospitable to one another; caring for one another; comforting one another; considering one another; edifying one another; exhorting one another; forgiving one another; giving preference to one another; greeting one another; having fellowship with one another; having compassion for one another; kindly affectionate to one another; like-minded toward one another; loving one another; members of one another; ministering gifts to one another; not judging one another; of the same mind toward one another; receiving one another; sending gifts to one another; serving one another; speaking to one another in psalms, hymns, and spiritual songs; submitting to one another; waiting for one another.

A picture of humble group commitment emerges from that collection. Every one of us should read that list every day before we deal with people. What would your family be like if that were its job description? What about your church? Your workplace?

I hear you. Immediately you think of all the reasons it won't happen. I do too. We can't dictate how the fellow in the next cubicle is going to behave, particularly if Christ is not in his heart. We can't change a teenage daughter's personality overnight, and as for church—well, most churches have their share of people who can't seem to handle *any* of the items on that list. But there is one place we can start: we can do it ourselves.

I believe one committed person can change any group. Just start being a member of the people you work with or live with, and see what happens. I know this for certain: I have been on dysfunctional teams and in failing organizations, but I've also been in places where the group is approaching the unity we are discussing. When you find people like that, you don't ever want to leave them. If you build an organization like that, people will be pounding on your door, begging to sign on.

Have you ever heard the story of Dunkirk? From a military point of view it may have been England's darkest hour during World War II. In 1940, Hitler was finishing off France and getting ready to move on Great Britain. The English army was pinned in at the French coast in the channel port of Dunkirk. One quarter of a million British soldiers and more than one hundred thousand Allied troops were exposed, ready for capture or outright slaughter. England's beleaguered navy had enough ships to rescue perhaps seventeen thousand men. That was all.

When Hitler's troops were within a few miles, rushing in for the kill, the Ragtag Armada showed up. It was the strangest, most mismatched collection of boats ever seen in a port: tugs and trawlers, fishing boats, sailboats, small lifeboats, pleasure yachts, an island ferry named the *Gracie Fields*, and even the America's Cup challenger *Endeavor*. None of them were military ships, and all of them were manned by civilians coming to the rescue. They loaded on as many human bodies as each vessel could possibly support. The motley crew of ships managed to save 338,682 men that day. Naval history was made in the most unlikely fashion.

Folks, we only think we have problems in our organizations. It is amazing what we can do when we all pull together for a common purpose. If a Ragtag Armada made of tugboats and rowboats could thwart the forces of Hitler, how could we doubt what we can do by devoting our motley selves to one another, particularly with the power and will of our mighty God?

WE GATHER TOGETHER

Of all the privileges God has given me, there are none I consider more precious or holy than the privilege of serving on teams of all kinds, from the family that raised me to the one I now lead, from my first competitive teams to the one whose roster I made in 2007, from the first church I ever joined to the one I'm in now, right down to the publishing team that is partnering with me in this book.

There are days when I feel like a sick goose if not a dead duck. I need to rotate to the back of the V, or I might even need to coast in for a landing and rest by a sunny pond. On those days I thank God for graciously giving me the people around me. On other days I try to remember that I need to have someone else's back. I really don't see how anyone can play Lone Ranger in this world of ours or in any world for that matter. Life is simply too tough for us *not* to try and build the tightest possible teams. And life is simply too wonderful and fruitful when we enjoy that beautiful sense of belonging.

In *The Return of the King*, the final film in the Lord of the Rings trilogy, Frodo the hobbit is trying to carry that evil ring to Mount Doom, where it can be safely destroyed. Nobody but Frodo can carry the ring. He has traveled a bit of the way with an amazing fellowship made of humans, hobbits, dwarves, and one wizard; now, however, it is just Frodo and his loving friend, Sam.

The final miles of the journey are terrible. The mountain is hideous and filled with monsters, and the ring is weighing heavier and heavier on Frodo. He feels so weak and discouraged that he questions whether he can go on. At every turn Sam is there to protect his friend, at times risking his life for Frodo.

Near the end Frodo lies in exhaustion as Sam cradles his head. Sam tries to cheer him up by reminding him of their home and of familiar and friendly things. "It will be spring soon," he says. "Do you remember the taste of strawberries and cream?"

"No, Sam," Frodo groans. "I can't recall the taste of food, the sound of water, the touch of grass. There's nothing."

Sam encourages Frodo to end the quest once and for all. He says, "Come on, Mr. Frodo. I can't carry it [the ring] for you. But I can carry *you*. Come on."[5]

Sam hoists Frodo onto his back and begins trudging up the mountain, where the goal will finally be reached. Sam was probably the least well-regarded member of the fellowship. But in the end he is the true hero. He understands what it means to be on a team and to be a member of someone else.

Can the same be said of you?

8

····

Identification: Fly Your Flag

So you think you are tough? Let's find out what you're made of. I'm going to send you straight into the line of fire.

Be forewarned—where I am sending you, tensions run high, people get nasty, and you will struggle to keep your composure. Hey, if you can't handle it, I'll understand.

Yes, I'm talking about volunteering for parking lot duty at your local church on Sunday morning.

Listen, I have been a fighter since my dad gave me boxing gloves when I was a kid. I was an old-school, hard-nosed football player, and I have spent a lot of my early years hanging out in taverns with roughnecks (oil field workers) who would fight you at the drop of a hat. But the church parking lot—that is a whole different level of hard knocks!

Let me tell you how I found out.

My church was experiencing a growth spurt during the eighties and early nineties. We needed new facilities, so we began an expansion campaign that was certain to cause inconvenience for nearly everyone. Construction of new buildings will do that because it gets in the way of parking spaces.

I volunteered for parking lot duty because I wasn't planning to teach a

Sunday school class that year. Hey, how tough could it be? This would be a chance to stand outdoors, get some fresh air, and direct people to the best remaining parking spaces while enjoying the morning sunshine.

We had a close-knit team. We met each Sunday for the first few weeks, making sure we all understood our assignments. After that we were on our own. Everybody had an assigned location and was responsible for getting a replacement if he or she couldn't be there.

During week two I had a question. As soon as the traffic died down and I got back to the meeting room, I asked, "Hey guys—is it just me, or are we finding out that we have some rude brothers and sisters in Christ at this church? Anybody else taking consistent abuse like I am?"

My question caused chaos to break out in the room. Everybody was telling a story at the same time.

"I got challenged to a fight!"

"I got flipped off!"

"About ten people rolled down their windows and shouted at me!"

"You think *that's* bad . . ."

Rude church members—the same ones who had come to this address to pray, sing hymns, study the Bible, and listen to sermons. What is wrong with this picture?

It was difficult not to respond when people lashed out at us. Some of us were struggling to keep our composure and not sink to the levels of the drivers. After all, we were there to serve our fellow members. Most of us had considered it an entry-level ministry task, but it looked as if parking lot duty required the patience of Job, the coolness of Daniel, and the temperament of Mother Teresa.

Our group dug in. Before heading out to the firing line, we would pray together. Then we would get down to brass tacks and discuss what in the world we were doing to catch such hostility from church members and visitors, who seemed like wonderful people in every place and in every time other than just before or after church in the parking lot. We talked about smiling more. We agreed to use a more accommodating tone of voice and to avoid being too authoritarian in our directions. We decided to ease up on the rules and be more flexible with drivers—and that was a bad idea.

When we gave an inch, they took a mile. Once we allowed the first car to drive through the orange cones that closed a lane, we may as well have removed all of the cones. "Hey, I saw the silver Buick do it!" We started to become very cynical about people, concluding that our church members would do whatever they could get away with—as long as they were behind a windshield and a steering wheel.

Then came a breakthrough. It is amazing how often big discoveries are made completely by accident.

A SITUATION WELL IN HAND

One Sunday morning I was running late. I got to church in time to take my post with the traffic but not to pray and strategize in advance. I got word to my buddies that I was on the job, but I headed right out to the parking lot instead of going to the meeting room, where normally I would have left my Bible. I had to hold it in my hand as I directed cars.

On this morning for some reason, it was as if, like in the NFL, we had suddenly traded with another church, getting a friendly congregation for a pipe organ and two church buses to be named later. Everybody smiled at me as I pointed them in the right direction. Nobody honked. No one wanted to fight, and a few people even lowered their windows and wished me a good morning. As I walked into the church, I realized how smoothly things had gone. Maybe it was the weather or something else; who knew?

As I directed postchurch traffic, it happened again! People waved and smiled warmly. One of the women asked me if I had held my Bible the entire session. I shrugged and said, "Sure, it's not too heavy." *What an odd question,* I thought.

Then another guy rolled his window down and asked the same thing. I answered him and wondered why the Bible in my hand was of so much interest to people.

When I entered the meeting room and asked the guys if they had noticed people being nicer, they stared at me. Absolutely not! They all said it was the same bad manners and angry treatment as usual. I said, "Well, people have been supernice to me. Many of them have even smiled and stopped to chat."

One guy immediately offered to trade assigned positions. He said he could use a smile or two.

I doubted whether one location was really a more ill-tempered one than another. That made no sense, especially since the friendly treatment had only occurred on this one morning. Suddenly it hit me what had happened; I know you figured it out several paragraphs ago.

"Folks," I said, "next week, every one of you needs to carry a Bible."

When they heard my stories, they thought it was a brilliant plan. A Bible! Who would have thought it? One of the guys wanted to buy bright orange Bible covers for the team, to match the cones, warning stickers, and flags. We found out that didn't work. It wasn't about carrying a book—it was about carrying *the* book.

From then on I took my leather-bound Bible with me every week and never had another bad experience in the parking lot. I just had to make sure that as I walked, I didn't leave a trail of little notes, bookmarks, church bulletins, and all the other residue we collect in our Bibles over the years.

That whole episode made such an impression on me that I wondered how it might work if I applied it in other places. After all, parking lots aren't the only locations where people let their hostility hang out, right? I decided that I would try carrying my Bible with me everywhere I went for three days.

Being the structured person I am, I had to establish some rules. The first rule was that I had to carry the book in my hand where it was plainly visible at all times. It couldn't be in a briefcase or book bag and no stuffing it up into my armpit. The whole point was visibility. If I needed both hands, I would lay it down beside me until I was ready to pick it up and move on.

The second rule was I might read my Bible at any time, but I would not initiate any conversations about it with anyone. I was going to leave it to God to send people and let *them* raise the issue. That's how talking about God works best. If someone asked me about the Bible, I would answer his question and talk with him based on his level of interest.

I need to add a disclaimer here. As I write these words, I have a mental picture of one of those window washers on a skyscraper. I hope he doesn't get the idea that I'm advising him to put a Bible into one of the two hands he needs for personal safety. This worked for me because both of my hands were often free. If you want to try it, carry your Bible when it's safe and appropriate, and be sure you keep it nearby where it won't be lost or stolen.

Would you like to hear what happened to me during those three days?

DOING THINGS BY THE BOOK

In the parking lot it seemed as if the visibility of a Bible had changed the behavior of others. What surprised me was that when I began carrying it around with me in other places, the person who behaved most differently was me.

I found that my conversations were more careful, more positive, and more constructive. I didn't attend a movie during those three days, but if I had, I might have chosen the subject much more carefully than usual. I had a far tighter focus on the things in life that please God. It's not as if I normally behaved in a way that wasn't godly, but I know that when I had his Word in my line of sight, I was a far better and more deliberately Christian human being.

As for other people, not too many of them approached me to ask about the Bible. One gentleman did want to know if I was a preacher. I told him I wasn't but that I loved God's Word and enjoyed having it with me. He told me that he was a fellow believer and that he was inspired by my boldness in carrying my Bible, simply to have it on my person.

The rest of the people in my path may not have broached the subject, but I felt that they behaved differently around me. People were more courteous and friendly and even more relaxed. The way things are in our current world, you might expect a visible Bible to be politically incorrect, and you might guess that it would cause people to feel awkward and to keep their distance. But I didn't find that to be true at all. I think people respect Christians who have the courage of their convictions. They know precisely where we stand, so whether they are believers or not, they are more likely to feel at ease around us.

When the three-day test ended, I had to leave on an extended trip. The little experiment was over, and I forgot about carrying a Bible—until recently.

Eileen and I moved from Texas back to Franklin, Tennessee, after the end of the 2007 football season. We found a perfect home in a nice Franklin subdivision. About a half mile from our house was a beautiful church on forty acres. A huge parking lot wrapped around the church, and the west side of the property extended down to the Harpeth River.

Someone from the church had a ten-foot cross erected beside the water. It is surrounded by beautiful oak trees with the ground covered in bark mulch. It is a beautiful place, and the presence of the cross adds to the loveliness of the landscape.

When I first saw the cross, I told Eileen how beautiful it was. Soon we began driving over to the church property for our daily walks, always stopping to pray beside the cross.

One day when Eileen was having ear and sinus problems, we talked about whether it would be wise for her to walk in the cold with the wind blowing as it was. I told her, "Well, it's kind of chilly. But if you bundle up really well, it might not be so bad."

She thought about it a moment and said, "Let me grab my Bible. If I find I can't handle it, I'll just sit in the truck and have my devotional time. Then you and Zoey [our bulldog] can go without me."

As we drove toward the church, the Bible in Eileen's lap reminded me of my experiment. It got me to thinking of God's Word in my hand. I had been thinking of trying it again, but this time for a longer period—say, seven days.

Sure enough, Eileen couldn't handle the cold. As I walked the dog, I continued to reflect on my experiment. I was envisioning things I might say to anyone who asked me why I carried a Bible. As I reached the back of the parking lot and started down the bark mulch trail leading to the cross, I began to pray aloud, "Lord, what would you have me say if someone asked me about my Bible?"

The answer seemed to pop into my head: "For I am not ashamed of the gospel of Christ, for it is the power of God to salvation for everyone who believes, for the Jew first and also for the Greek" (Romans 1:16).

I hadn't thought about that verse in years. I reflected carefully upon it as I stood holding on to the cross and looking at the beautiful Harpeth River. I asked God to give me an assurance that he had put that Bible verse in my mind. I didn't want it to be about me. I asked him to use my wife, Eileen, to deliver some confirmation to me.

I walked back to the truck and helped Zoey jump into the backseat. I settled in at the wheel beside my wife and asked her how her devotional time had gone. "I really enjoyed it," she smiled. She had actually stuffed a little devotional magazine into her Bible. It had a nice story about a burglar who had stolen a Bible, along with some other stuff, and was converted by a verse he read as he rolled the pages into cigarettes.

"That's a great story," I told Eileen after she had related it in detail. "Did it mention what verse finally got to him?"

She said, "The verse was Romans 1:16."

I quickly pulled the truck to the side of the road, parked it, and let the tears come. I felt uncontrollable emotion. Eileen, of course, couldn't imagine what was going on. I explained to her what had gone on between God and me, how that very verse had come into my mind and how I had asked God to confirm my impression through her. She was just as amazed, and we were both excited by how God had used us together.

RAISING YOUR BANNER

That story required several paragraphs to tell, but it's necessary for making this point: soldiers fight with better resolve when they carry a flag into battle. Have you seen those old pictures of the infantry charging with the battle flag raised high and at the front? I have always been inspired by the story of the raising of the flag at Iwo Jima. The famous photograph was taken as the flag was hoisted on the one high peak on that little island. It took some time to capture the island afterward, but the sight of the flag inspired the soldiers to risk their lives for their goal.

Think of the Bible as your flag as you go out into the world. It serves as a visible symbol to others, but in particular, it reminds you of the cause for which you are living. I had thought the point of my experiment was how other people would respond to the sight. Sure enough, I have had some wonderful opportunities to talk about my faith when people saw God's Word in my hands. But the real point is how I myself behave when the Scriptures are on my person.

It's like putting on my team colors before a game. When I used to do that, I connected emotionally to the idea of team and common goals. By carrying the Bible, I have boldly and unmistakably identified myself, and that is a transforming experience.

When Paul wrote those words, "I'm not ashamed of the gospel," he was speaking to a young church about his eagerness to come serve it. He was busy preaching to all kinds of people in different cities, and quite often he was dealing with hostility and even physical danger. But Paul was saying, "The gospel is my power base." He wasn't going to hide his affiliation with a Savior who had died for his sins. He wasn't going to run away from the conflicts that arose when he spoke the name of Christ. He lived one of the most remarkable lives of history and changed the Western world forever, simply by identifying his cause in his own mind and then boldly standing behind it. When he entered a new city, he wasted no time in finding the public meeting place and standing up to tell everyone what he was all about.

Sometimes as I stood on the sideline at a football game, I would take a look at the crowd. At a college game the student section is always the rowdiest. If you have watched a few games on television, you know that college kids go all out to support their teams. They dress in crazy costumes, paint their bodies with team colors, and shout their lungs out. Sometimes right in the middle of those wild rows of rabid fans, I would spot some brave soul wearing the colors of the *other* team. This visiting fan would be catching all kinds of grief! If the home team scored, he would be taunted unmercifully by everyone around him. Some fan behavior, unfortunately, can even become dangerous. But football lovers support their teams. They wear the paraphernalia, they shout their cheers, and they even venture into *enemy* territory if they end up with a ticket that sends them there.

That's the way you and I need to be—not just with the Bible or some other token of our spiritual faith but with every affiliation that means something to us. We draw power and inspiration from identifying with a cause. If that is who you are, why not lift your flag and let the world know? This is about boldly presenting yourself in public.

Let's talk about the power base known as identification.

DARE TO BE YOURSELF

One of the first lessons we teach our children is not to try to be something they are not. They read children's books that teach the lesson, *be yourself.*

It seems so obvious, but as I look around at people today, I see a lot of role confusion, don't you? Some people crave acceptance, and they are afraid of being rejected if they let others see who they are and where they stand. We have already talked about the faith side of things, and that is a very obvious place where we run into this problem. In this day and age there are some settings where it is not politically correct to be a Christian.

Maybe you are a guy with a new job in a new office, and none of your coworkers strike you as people who attend church or spend much time in prayer. What if they find out you are a devout Christian? Will they ostracize you?

You would make a great mistake by giving in to that fear and hiding your identity. For one thing, we can't be ashamed of the gospel when someone gave his life to bring it to us. But also, if we hide our light under a bushel, we miss incredible opportunities to minister to other people. It could be that the very reason God has placed you in that office is so that you can change somebody's life. Jesus said, "You are the light of the world . . . Let your light so shine before men" (Matthew 5:14–16). That's what we are talking about here.

Let me tell you how some men and women approach this issue in the business world. First of all, they keep a Bible sitting on their desks. That's right; they do exactly what I did, but they simply keep the book in reach where business associates can see it. Guess what that's called? Raising a flag. The beauty of it is that you don't need to say a word. The Word itself is worth a thousand of them. Coworkers see your Bible and know something very important about you, without your having to grope awkwardly for some way to raise the subject. Your flag is at full mast on your desk, and you have quietly sent a message.

The second thing believers do once they have gotten to know people and have gently demonstrated their identity as believers is to tell a faith story. How does that work? You simply wait for the right moment to arise, then demonstrate a Christian response to the subject that has been raised. Begin by praying for such a moment, saying, "God, I want an opportunity to help that person who has come into my heart lately. I believe you are paving the way for me to talk to him. Please give me an opportunity to share a faith story."

Then listen closely when your friend speaks. If he or she brings up a problem, you have the opportunity to say something like, "You know, one thing that has helped me in that situation is an idea from the Bible." Or you can tell how God answered a past prayer; say whatever is appropriate.

You are not being pushy or aggressive, just responding to a conversational cue. You are giving a bite-size serving of your testimony, and that is the most convincing form of faith sharing there is. People can say they don't believe in God, but they can't argue with the experience of your life. Sharing a faith story is just more personal than having the Bible on your desk.

The third and most critical step, after you have done well with the first two, is to find the opportunity to share the gospel with your friend. Ask God to give you the words, and he will do it every time. You will be amazed at how he will speak through you. Of course, you will want to have done your homework for such a moment, through prayer and through learning how to lead someone to Christ. It is not nearly as difficult as most people think. All you need to do is be available, know the simple basics of the plan of salvation, and trust God to bring you to the right moment. There is nothing in this world more pleasing or joyful than seeing someone become a child of God.

You can see miracles of ministry happen in your life, but they will only happen if you go public—if you raise your flag.

Dare to be yourself, and let Christ shine through you.

DARE TO BE TRANSPARENT

The second principle of being yourself is to be transparent. What am I getting at here? I've talked about identification, about saying to the world, "This is who I am—take me or leave me—and I'm not ashamed of it." That is not arrogance; that is simple honesty.

We live in a world in which people wear all kinds of masks. They may raise flags, but they are not showing their true colors. I have been around a whole lot of guys, of course, given my career in strength and conditioning, and I know that the macho facade is very often a carefully cultivated mask. We teach males that they are supposed to be tough, independent, and mysterious. We don't teach them much about showing their true feelings. But what is it that others find truly refreshing and irresistible? Transparency.

When you carry your Bible, wear your colors, or take some other action to show the world who you are, that is the beginning. The Bible is a label, and it is a highly significant one. Carrying your Bible should be the beginning of sharing with other people exactly who you are.

Psychologists tell us that patient after patient come into their offices and say, "You're the first person I've ever been really honest with." Think about that. Most of us know hundreds of people. How can we get so far in life without being truly honest with at least a couple of very close friends? Yet you and I both know that it is quite common.

The more secretive we become and the more closed off we are, the less power we have in life. A mask is not a power base but a power drain.

Notice what Jesus said to his disciples: "No longer do I call you servants, for a servant does not know what his master is doing; but I have called you friends, for all things that I heard from My Father I have made known to you" (John 15:15). Jesus is telling us his idea of a friend: someone who tells you everything.

As you move forward with your life, be certain you have dropped your masks. I found that carrying my Bible was a way of getting comfortable at showing the world who I was. It was one thing to seek God in quiet solitude, but it felt good to let the world know how much I love my Lord. Why would you or I be nervous about putting that Bible down on a restaurant table or carrying it through the lobby of an airport? Could it be a transparency problem? Are we so afraid of rejection that it becomes easier to keep quiet about our faith?

My advice is to forget the risk. Life is unfulfilling when lived in caution or fear, so go for it! Let people know where you stand. With those people closest to you, be honest and transparent. Share who you really are and how you feel. And as you meet new people, don't be reserved. Let them know exactly who you are and what you stand for.

Psychologists tell us that the more transparent people are, the more likely they are to attract new friends. As a matter of fact, some counselors will begin an appointment with a new client by personally sharing something about themselves. As soon as they become transparent, they find their clients are likely to return the intimacy by opening up themselves. You will find the same thing. By hedging your bets and keeping quiet, you will accomplish exactly the thing you are trying so hard to avoid: you will encourage people to pull away from you.

But if you share who you really are, others will quickly feel comfortable and at ease around you. Soon you will have a new friendship to strengthen your life, which is what this power base is all about.

DARE TO BE STRONG AND COURAGEOUS

Joshua was one of the greatest leaders in the Bible. He took over for Moses, and his job was to lead the Israelites into the land that God had promised them as their birthright. Joshua must have been at least a little nervous. Not only was Moses a hard act to follow, but even under that great man's leadership, the Israelites ended up wandering in the wilderness for forty years.

God basically told Joshua not to sweat it. He said to the new leader:

Be strong and of good courage, for to this people you shall divide as an inheritance the land which I swore to their fathers to give them. Only be strong and very courageous . . . Have I not commanded you? Be strong and of good courage; do not be afraid, nor be dismayed, for the LORD your God is with you wherever you go. (Joshua 1:6–7, 9)

Did you notice one phrase that keeps popping up in that text? "Be strong and of good courage" or some form of those words. If God said it three times, we know there must have been a good reason for it. The writers of the ancient Scriptures used repetition for emphasis—to pound a point home, much as a preacher might do today. From what I can tell, these words appear to be the first locker-room speech in history. In the locker room good coaches motivate the team and get the adrenaline pumping so that the players are ready to run out onto the field and perform like champions.

Israel had been stuck in the middle of nowhere for four decades. They had spent nearly forty years completing what was actually a march of a few days. Why? They lacked faith. They lacked courage. They did not understand the implication of having God on their side, even with all he had done for them. Therefore, God told Joshua to tell the people to be confident in the knowledge that they would have his presence and his power. Why should they be anything but strong and courageous?

It wasn't long before Joshua was leading his people across the river and directing them to take the territory that had been their legacy for so long. Guess what? The Israelites raised their flags. The Bible tells us that they always carried their banners in the wilderness: one for each of the tribes of Israel. When they were fighting, the Bible tells us the soldiers rallied beneath their banners. I find it exciting that Isaiah told us that one day we would have a Lord (Jesus Christ) who would "stand as a banner to the people" (Isaiah 11:10).

No wonder we can dare to be strong and courageous. We can knock down the walls as Joshua did at Jericho. There is no barrier too great for us, no task that is impossible, when we march forward in God's will, bearing our banners in the knowledge that he is with us wherever we go.

So put these ideas together. You are going to march forward with a strong sense of identity, unafraid to show the world who you are. Meanwhile, you are not going to be arrogant or deceptive about it; you will always be honest and transparent, traits that others find attractive. Finally, you will be as bold and assertive as you are open and forthcoming.

I think you can imagine how successful an individual with these attributes would be. What we have just described is the blueprint for leadership. Yet there is one more trait that I consistently identify with effective achievers and leaders: the ability to listen.

DARE TO LISTEN

Imagine I am carrying my Bible in public again. I walk into a restaurant, sit down, and place that Bible on the table before me. I am flying my flag. A waiter walks over to take my order, and he greets me. "My name is George, and I will be your server today," he says. "How are you?"

I am being transparent, too, so I say, "Thanks for asking, George. I am doing very well though I am worried about a good friend of mine. I spent several minutes praying for him this morning."

The waiter smiles and says, "I did notice your Bible. So what would you like to ..."

Before he can finish asking about my beverage, I show that I am also strong and courageous. With great confidence I say, "Prayer is very important to me. I spend time each day talking with God, bringing him my requests and experiencing his wonderful presence. At the same time, I study this Bible that you see beside me. I'm reading through it again, from Genesis to Revelation, and right now I am up to the book of Leviticus."

I go on and on like that as the waiter begins to glance around the room in increasing discomfort. He has been assigned to eight tables, of which this is one, and several other tables need his attention. I continue to talk on and on.

Notice that I have faithfully followed all of the guidelines we have discussed in this chapter. I have established my identity and been my true self. I have been transparent, and I have been bold and assertive. What's missing? Obviously I'm not going to be too successful in this instance because I have no awareness of the other person in the conversation. I need to listen to not only his words but also his body language. He shouldn't even have to tell me he has other tables. It is common knowledge, but he reminds me when he glances at some of those other customers.

This chapter is really about boldness, particularly the boldness to be ourselves and declare who we really are. But a lot of people do that and make a big mess. Paul said, "Though I speak with the tongues of men and of angels, but have not love, I have become sounding brass or a clanging cymbal" (1 Corinthians 13:1). In other words, you can be the world's most persuasive speaker, but without love for the listener, you are just making a whole lot of noise.

Have you ever known someone like that? Who would you rather be around: a quiet but sensitive person or a lively but insensitive one? The quiet one is going to win that popularity contest every time. The New Testament writer James said, "Let every man be swift to hear, slow to speak" (James 1:19), which goes along with the old saying that God gave you two ears and one mouth for a reason. Therefore, if you want to be heard, you must first learn how to hear. Listening is a dying art in this world in which everyone wants to get a word in edgewise. Particularly as we speak about our faith, we need to "earn the right to be heard." That means showing through our behavior that our words are worth someone else's attention.

Even with a stranger it is possible to do that. Show courtesy to everyone you meet. Smile and mean it. Ask questions before seeking any attention of your own. And when someone speaks to you, know that you are being honored by having the thoughts of one of God's children bestowed upon you. Listen attentively, without interrupting. Ask follow-up questions. Make brief statements that show you have heard and have sympathized.

If transparency is a surefire way to build new friendships, listening is even more effective. Transparency is about how you share yourself, but listening is about how you encourage others to do so. The combination, of course, is a menu for a vast army of admirers.

You can be that rarest of people—a bold, courageous, flag-carrying good listener.

PUTTING IT ALL TOGETHER

Here is a good exercise. Take a sheet of paper, write the numbers one through five, and next to each number write a word or short phrase that identifies who you are. For example, *man* or *woman* would be an identifier—and since I suggested it, you can't use that one. I would rather you be more specific anyway. List the first important self-labels that come to mind. Those of us in the work world tend to put our careers at the top of the list. When we meet people at parties, the first thing we ask for is a name, which is the ultimate identifier. And our next question is "What do you do?" That is, what is your line of work?

That, too, is a key identifier. Your faith might be one item on the list, and your family position might be another. There are a hundred ways you could describe yourself, only a few of which are highly significant to you. You will have no problem thinking of five good ones. What is most important is what you put at the top of your list because your first reaction is an indicator of how you see yourself. It was very important to me to carry my Bible in public because the first item on my list would be *follower of Jesus Christ*. But this principle of flag carrying is broader than that. The idea is to be bold about identifying who you are.

Let's say you are a tax accountant, and that is very important to you. Am I suggesting you walk around with a thick copy of the tax code? Well, not necessarily—not unless you want people to flee! On the other hand, if you are excited about what you do, you will find ways to identify yourself to others and show your passion for the world of tax accounting. Your passion is your true flag. You can raise it by telling that restaurant waiter, "I just attended a terrific seminar in tax accounting."

Don't laugh! My point is, if you are emotionally invested in what you do, people will always be interested and their interest doesn't stand or fall on the subject itself—it rests on your feelings about it.

Simply stated, passionate, flag-waving human beings are fascinating to others. As a matter of fact, they can cause whole movements. People (particularly younger ones) will follow their career paths simply because passion is contagious and seductive. We need to be attractive followers of Christ, attractive tax accountants, attractive window washers, parents, spouses, or whatever it is that galvanizes us to live in this world.

This is why I say to you, raise your flag! Hold it high and proudly, and don't fight back that grin. Not only is it going to launch hundreds of fascinating new friendships, but it is going to reignite your own love for the subject as you find others tuning in. Remember the effect on my own behavior of simply having a Bible in my hands.

John Wesley once said, "Set yourself on fire, and people will come for miles to watch you burn." That's what a flag is really all about, isn't it? It is a colorful banner that no one can fail to see, and it reads, "Adventure is to be found just below this cloth!"

Why not start a fire and draw a crowd?

9

Adversity: Turn Your Difficulties to Your Advantage

Some wise guy once told me, "Hey, I'm not perfect. Several years ago I thought I'd made a mistake, but it turned out I was wrong."

We don't enjoy discussing the occasions when we have bungled things. I know I have contributed more than my share to the great human pool of foul-ups. It took a few years of maturing before I could regularly stand in front of the mirror and admit to myself that I was prone to messing up. And I had to travel a little further on the path of maturity before I could freely discuss my shortcomings with people I knew well.

Finally, the real test: as a public speaker I had to "man up" and tell an audience of strangers all about my many wrong turns on the highway of life. But I did that and survived. I even found I could write about them.

Through honest confession (to myself and others), something wonderful happened. Not only did I get the second chance to fulfill my dreams, but God has seen fit to use my story to help other people through their own regrets and redemption scenarios. It feels good to know that God could serve so much lemonade from the lemons my tree produced.

As human beings, we come in all shapes, sizes, and varieties. But there are two things we all have in common. First, we are flawed creations. Second, God loves us anyway, and he wants to put us on the road toward becoming better, less mistake-prone people.

Can you think of a time when you have really dropped the ball? Could you name the single biggest mistake you have made thus far, and more important, are you comfortable discussing it?

Here is the better question: Have you been able to observe the good things that emerged from your trials and tribulations? This is an incredibly crucial power base for any life. If you can look back at the worst moments and see the parts they played in building your best moments, you are going to be energized by the principle that in human experience nothing is ever wasted.

This is a deeply Christian principle, of course, but I believe it is something nearly everyone can observe and understand. You can either call it the Romans 8:28 outlook ("All things work together for good to those who love God") or just the school of hard knocks. Either way, most of us can learn to study the wrong moves we have made and see that genuine wisdom resulted or perhaps opportunities that wouldn't have occurred otherwise.

As a parent and grandparent, I have thought quite a bit about preparing children to deal with failure. How exactly do we teach that? So often we observe, for many people, experience is the only effective teacher. We would love to follow our children through life and warn them of every danger and every bad decision, but we know we can't do that. We also know that they are going to have to stumble occasionally, or they will never internalize certain lessons. Even so, I wanted my kids to know how to work through their problems with a positive attitude, to learn to bounce back, and to embrace their tough times as teachable moments.

Unfortunately not all parents do a good job of that. Perhaps they have been hard on themselves, but they are also very hard on their kids: "See, I told you! Look at the mess you have made. You were bound to screw up!" Negative parenting has an echo effect. When we repeatedly say certain things to our children, the statements become embedded in their subconscious. Even after we are no longer around, they will hear those tapes playing. That is why we should make them positive, affirming, inspiring tapes.

I have learned a wonderful truth through this whole experience. It is incredibly satisfying to let our children (or anyone else) get the benefit of the mistakes in our past. If you have kids, have you showed them where you went wrong once upon a time and how God has used your struggle?

I know what you are going to say: "Oh, my kids don't listen to me. They think my childhood was during the Stone Age, and that it has nothing to do with today."

Sure, it seems that way at times. But they hear far more than you think. Don't you remember how many words and ideas you soaked in from your own parents even when they thought you were paying no attention? I do. I listened far more than they ever realized, and I internalized so much of their advice.

We have the opportunity to say to our kids or to others who might listen, "Look, you're bound to mess up, just as I did. But you know what is wonderful? No failure is final; nothing is ever wasted. And as much as we enjoy peaceful times, those teach us nothing, while hardship distills true wisdom. Let me give you an example . . ."

If you are anything like me, you have a whole library of pain and progress to draw upon. The wisdom we receive is like gold, but passing it on to others invests that gold in a way that may well pay dividends from now until the end of time. Your children will draw on your stories, pass on that wisdom to their children, and so on. It is an issue of legacy. This is why I am no longer hesitant to share my bungles in cringe-inducing detail. Books such as *The Senior* and, to a lesser extent, this one only multiply the results. I think about all the readers who might be able to see where I went wrong, and I get very excited.

Let me tell you a story from our local community that shows what happens when wisdom is passed along.

"YOU SAVED MY LIFE"

Like so many people today, I meet friends and associates in a lot of public places—coffee shops, diners, hotel lobbies. Recently I was in downtown Franklin, Tennessee, for a casual meeting with an associate of mine. We were deeply involved in conversation when I noticed a man standing a few feet away. I had only vaguely noticed this fellow in my peripheral vision as he walked to the counter to pick up his order.

On his way back to wherever he was sitting, he had stopped in his tracks a few feet from our table. His eyes were wide, and he was looking in my direction. I looked up and made eye contact with him and offered a polite smile. The man then walked over to our table. "May I ask your name?" he said tentatively to me.

I stood, offered my hand, and said that I was Mike Flynt.

Now he looked pleased. "I knew it!" he said. "Mike Flynt! I can't believe I'm actually getting the chance to meet you."

Though puzzled, I smiled again and nodded for him to continue. He told me that he was new in town. He had brought his family to Franklin from San Diego, California.

"Back in December I was in a very dark place in my life," he said grimly. "I had been depressed for a long time, and I couldn't seem to see any light at the end of the tunnel. When I hit bottom, I placed a hose in the tailpipe of my car. I was going to put the other end through my window in the driver's seat, breathe in the fumes, and let my life slip into oblivion. First I walked back into the house, thinking over my decision for one last time. As I passed through the family room, the television was on—and your face was on it. It was some talk show in Dallas."

"That would be the *Joni* show," I said. Joni Lamb has a talk show on the Daystar network, and I knew that was where he most likely saw me.

"Yeah," he said. "That was it! So anyway, you were talking about how you had reached a bad place in your own life. You didn't feel there was anything left to do but end it. Of course, when I heard those words, it was as if you were talking directly to me. I sat down and started listening."

I was listening, too, with awe.

"You told your story about how you thought about taking your life, and you showed your pain," he said. "I could see from your face that it was real. But you told how God had delivered you from the choice of suicide. After that was over, I laid facedown on the floor and began praying, 'If you can do it for Mike, you can do it for me.'"

This man's voice was trembling, and I could see he was close to tears. He said, "I walked outside and pulled the hose out of my tailpipe. I kept on talking to God, and I haven't stopped from that day to this one. And now God has led me across your path so that I can say *thank you!* You played a huge role in saving my life."

You know what? I can't remember much about the meeting that brought me to that bakery. I'm sure it was very important. But never in my life will I ever forget the experience of coming across a complete stranger who told me I had played a part in saving his life.

It's a curious thing. When I was a football player, my performance had an immediate payoff. I could see the fans dressed in team colors, and I could hear them rock the stadium with their cheering. If I made a tackle, there was the instant gratification of crowd approval.

Then as I walked across the campus, people would come up and talk about the game. If I were to do something else in front of a live audience, such as sing or act in a play, I would hear the applause. But writing a book is entirely different. I'm not likely to meet most of the people who read these words. It is the same with appearing on TV or radio. I might have gone my whole life without knowing something I said contributed to that man's decision to keep living—which is far more important than anything that happens on a football field or a theatrical stage.

There are times when I get discouraged and think, *What's the use? Who wants to read a book by me anyway?* Or *Why do I bother with these speaking engagements? I enjoy speaking, but does it really change anything?*

I have learned not to take anything for granted. God weaves a tapestry of human events; its threads are very fine, they are wound in very complex patterns, and they stretch across this whole globe and into the future. We never know how our actions affect other people. If you have seen the movie *It's a Wonderful Life*, you have seen a beautiful parable about how this process works. You could do some small thing tomorrow—you might say some word or make some gesture—that seems meaningless to you but could have an incredible impact on someone else's life. God ties it all up together, and we see only the smallest part of how it all works out. When you and I get to heaven, we will be able to stand back and study the whole tapestry. One of my great hopes is that I will be happy with the influences I had.

God did save me from a tragic decision at one time. By his grace I decided to keep going. But what if? What if I had known my decision would one day dramatically affect someone else's life?

If I had understood the consequences of my actions and how God uses events, I wouldn't have even come close to doing what I almost did. I would have understood that because of this principle, there is always hope. There is never an occasion for giving up, and, in fact, there are solid reasons to feel good about bad experiences.

God is going to use your adversity. Believe me on this. Let's look at how it happens.

THE MEANING OF ADVERSITY

We are going to confront things we can't change; therefore, we must allow them to change us.

It doesn't matter who you are, how much power you have, how many official friends you have on Facebook, or how much money is in your bank account. If you have a pulse, you are going to struggle, and struggle is not going to be a rare thing. It is simply what life has been like on this planet ever since Adam and Eve got a craving for that forbidden fruit.

Each age and stage of life brings its own problems. Remember what constituted a crisis when you were ten years old? It was something like a rained-out playdate. When you got to be a teenager, it might have been the cute member of the opposite sex who never noticed you. In adulthood, the problems became much more significant and serious. Still, whatever your age there have always been obstacles, trials, and problems. And at each stage they helped you learn something about yourself and about life.

When we view failure as a power base in our lives, we begin seeing problems as stepping-stones rather than stumbling blocks. If you could see your life from the eternal perspective, you would see your darkest moments as your holiest ones, for they were the ones that brought you true wisdom. They were the times that caused you to reach deep within yourself and find what it took to keep going. On those occasions, if you were truly wise, you reached out to God.

The New Testament teaches us the following truth:

My brethren, count it all joy when you fall into various trials, knowing that the testing of your faith produces patience. But let patience have its perfect work, that you may be perfect and complete, lacking nothing. (James 1:2–4)

I think you will agree that the person who can be joyful in a time of trial has harnessed an amazing power. Many people read this verse and say, "Is this really possible? Are you telling me I should be laughing and joking on the day I lose my job or when something terrible happens in my family?"

No, of course not. The distinction is the difference between happiness and joy. Nobody is happy all the time. That is an emotion that comes and goes with the rise and fall of circumstances in life. I have happy days and sad ones, just like you.

But joy is something else entirely—it is not an emotion but a *policy*. It's like the difference between romantic affection and godly love. I love my wife and usually in a romantic sense. But not always. Sometimes, truth be told, we get on each other's nerves. On those occasions neither of us feels much romantic affection. But we have a deep, unbreakable policy of loving and supporting one another, in sickness and in health, in good times, and in times when we get on each other's nerves. We know that if we ride it out, the romantic part will come back.

It is the same way with happiness and joy. When you truly trust God and you feel that life has meaning rather than being a random and purposeless series of events, you are joyful about that, deep down, even when you are not particularly happy. You have made a decision, established a contract with the universe, set a policy of joy about life. You see, it's like knowing the ending of a book. It may look bad for the hero on page 100, but you know for a fact that he is going to live happily ever after on the final page. As God's child, you actually have that same incredible assurance. Bad things are going to happen, and there is no way to be happy about them. But in your heart and soul, you can be joyful because of what James has said—these things are making you "perfect and complete," lacking nothing.

A MEETING WITH ADVERSITY

The truth is, I know a lot of good people who *say* they believe all this stuff about strength through adversity. It's not exactly a new idea, is it?

There are people who have heard all the sermons, read the best books, and come to understand how this process is supposed to work. You go through life, you take your bumps and bruises, and it all works out in your favor before you reach the finish line. But I wonder how many people in their heart of hearts really stake their lives and attitudes on this truth?

Watch people when they face tough times, and you will find out. We often see people abandon their faith because God allowed something bad to happen to them. "If there is a God," they say, "where is he? I just can't believe that if he's there and if he cares about me, he would let me go through this." A massive number of books have been written on the subject of why bad things happen to good people. (Most of us are surprisingly quick to put ourselves into the *good* category, but that's another subject.)

The short answer is that God allows us to suffer because he loves us. He knows it is the only way we can grow. Sometimes we bring our own problems upon ourselves and have to learn our lessons the hard way. Often we make the same mistake again and again until we have to suffer consequences for our poor choices. It is then that we learn the benefits of discipline. Here is what the Bible has to say about it:

> So hold on through your sufferings, because they are like a father's discipline. God is treating you as children. All children are disciplined by their fathers . . . Our fathers on earth disciplined us for a short time in the way they thought was best. But God disciplines us to help us, so we can become holy as he is. We do not enjoy being disciplined. It is painful at the time, but later, after we have learned from it, we have peace, because we start living in the right way. (Hebrews 12:7, 10–11 NCV)

Sometimes we bungle things, but other times we aren't to blame; other people bring those problems upon us. But then, too, there is wisdom to be attained through suffering.

Most people go through hard times and ask God how he could allow it. But what is interesting is that when they go through good times, they never ask God whether they deserve those! We labor under the delusion that we are wonderful people who deserve nothing but an endless supply of fresh blessings. When Job, that long-suffering character in the Old Testament, was going through his hard times, his wife wondered why he didn't desert his faith. She actually advised him to "curse God and die."

His response to her was brilliant: "Should we take only good things from God and not trouble?" (Job 2:10 NCV).

Some people, then, cannot find God in adversity. Others find him more intimately there than in any other place. C. S. Lewis said, "God whispers to us in our pleasures, speaks to us in our conscience, but shouts in our pains: It is His megaphone to rouse a deaf world."[1] The way you meet adversity will be a watershed moment in your life. It will bring bitterness, which is like a slow cancer to the soul, or it will bring the very quiet joy of new wisdom and strength. It will cause you to conclude that God has no time for you, or it will bring you to experience just the opposite: a God who takes us into his loving arms and dries our tears.

The psalmist wrote, "Those who sow in tears shall reap in joy" (Psalm 126:5). That's a statement of the system that runs this world. We invest in suffering, and we receive dividends of new strength and better understanding.

So how will you meet adversity the next time? Nobody expects you to treat it as a picnic. But if you can see it for what it is—a chance to become more perfect and complete than you were yesterday—you will have taken in your hands a true power base, the power of strength through the refining fire.

Let's look at the good things that come out of bad times.

DEEPER WISDOM

When you are riding high in life and you have the world on a string, you tend to simply enjoy yourself, right? You don't think much about things. It would never occur to you to stop and ask God if he is sure you deserve all this good fortune. It just seems as if your life is exactly the way it is *supposed* to be. You just go with the flow, and that is why no wisdom comes out of the experience. Good times have their own reward, and that reward endures only insofar as it makes for a good memory.

But eventually you go off the path. You hit that bump in the road, you take a wrong turn, or maybe you have a painful collision with someone else on the highway of life. Suddenly you are doing much more thinking than you did while you were cruising along. You have to use your noggin during these times because thinking is necessary for adjustments. How are you going to get out of this ditch and back on the road? What changes should be made?

But hardship makes philosophers of us all, so you also ask yourself deeper questions: Why is life like this? Why do we all have so many problems? Did I do something to cause this, and if so, how can I avoid this pain in the future?

Notice that the wiser you are, the better the questions you will ask. (Foolish questions include, who can I blame this on? or why is God always picking on me? That kind of thing.)

The more times we go off the road, the better we get at asking the right questions. And that is what we call *wisdom*, my friend. It doesn't begin with answers, as you'd expect; it begins with questions—the right ones. Your adversity, if you invest it wisely, will yield a bumper crop of wisdom for your life. You will learn about yourself, you will learn about the world, and you will learn about God.

When you have a bad day, you can treat it with a certain sense of humor, like the guy who says, "I've learned from my mistakes, and today I made giant strides toward a PhD." If you think the world is a random and meaningless series of events, you are not likely to laugh very much—bad stuff is just bad stuff. But if you believe that bad stuff is an investment, that is a different matter. You now know that you are investing into this thing called wisdom, and you can follow it and put more resources into that, just as you would with any investment.

If you read the Bible closely, you will discover this fact: every person God ever used in a big way had a wilderness experience to survive first.

- Abraham had to wait decades for God to keep the promise to give him a son; furthermore, he had to pull up stakes and move to a hostile land. Then he became the father of a nation that blessed the world.

- Jacob had to flee the wrath of his brother, Esau; make his own way among strangers; and generally let life drum the foolishness out of him. Then he became a patriarch.
- Joseph had to sit in prison after being accused of a crime he didn't commit. Then he saved the nation of Egypt.
- Moses had to hide in the mountains and live as a shepherd, after being raised as a prince. Then he led the Israelites from slavery to independence.
- David spent years living in caves, staying away from jealous King Saul. Then he became Israel's greatest king.
- Jesus and Paul both had their wilderness periods before God would bring fruit to their lives.

If none of these men—not even Jesus—were exempt from hardship, then you can expect the same rule to apply in your life. As a matter of fact, you don't have to go to the Bible to see that pattern. Study the early failures of Abraham Lincoln or of nearly any great leader in any field, and you will find the wilderness before the wisdom. Just realize that everyone has struggles, but not everyone gains from them. You have to realize your investment and make it pay off.

In time it will pay dividend after dividend. And if wisdom were wealth, we all would have the opportunity to be Bill Gates.

PATIENCE AND PERSEVERANCE

Paul tells us this about our problems: "We also have joy with our troubles, because we know that these troubles produce patience. And patience produces character, and character produces hope" (Romans 5:3–4 NCV). That is a word picture of the manufacturing line of wisdom, isn't it? It's a chain reaction of blessings that spring from adversity. And isn't it interesting that, just as James does, Paul associates joy with hardship.

The first fruit is patience, and that is the gift no one is eager to earn. To be young is to be impatient. We live with all the energy of our youth, and we move at a fast pace. Not only that but today's world is all about instant gratification—fast food, quick computers, and get-rich-quick schemes. People have stopped believing that good things come to those who wait.

Adversity is all about coming to a brick wall and wanting to be on the other side. At first we are simply frustrated. We want the brick wall removed. It doesn't move on its own, so we beat our head against it a few times. All that accomplishes is a couple of concussions and a few ugly bumps on the forehead. So we try climbing over the wall, we try going around it, we attempt to dig under it, and eventually we come up with the right formula for removing the obstacle, or perhaps we are forced to move in some other direction. Time is required to work it all out, and impatience just causes us to make the wrong decisions. We need patience and persistence to make the right life adjustment.

U.S. president Calvin Coolidge once said, "Nothing in the world can take the place of Persistence. Talent will not; nothing is more common than unsuccessful men with talent. Genius will not; unrewarded genius is almost a proverb. Education will not; the world is full of educated derelicts. Persistence and determination alone are omnipotent. The slogan 'Press On' has solved and always will solve the problems of the human race."[2]

Many years ago a young man, Glenn Cunningham, was to start a fire in the stove of the local school every school day with the help of his brother. One day the two brothers poured on what they thought was kerosene. What they didn't know was that someone had mistakenly put gasoline into the can instead. The resulting explosion killed Glenn's brother and severely burned his own legs.

The doctors wanted to amputate Glenn's legs immediately, but the parents asked for a postponement to pray about it. Day after day the doctor asked for a decision, and the parents would not agree to the surgery. They were stubborn seekers of the will of God, and for two months they prayed for healing, meanwhile teaching Glenn to believe he would walk again.

The legs were never amputated, but when the bandages came off, one leg was three inches shorter than the other, and the toes on the left foot were all but gone. No one but Glenn and his parents thought he could ever walk again. Every day he put himself through grueling exercise and self-therapy—quite a feat considering this was 1917, when medical advances were nothing like what they are today. Still Glenn managed to get to a point of walking with the aid of crutches. Eventually he threw the crutches away. Then, miracle of miracles, he began running. It would have been a fantastic story even if it had ended there. But it didn't.

You might have a hard time believing this, but Glenn eventually set a world record in the mile run. During the thirties Glenn Cunningham was known as the World's Fastest Human Being. In 1978, he was named Athlete of the Century at a ceremony at Madison Square Garden.

The question is, did the explosion decrease or somehow actually *increase* his chances of becoming the world's top track athlete? At the point of adversity, you would have said the former, and you might have been willing to stake all your possessions on that proposition. At the finish line you would have to look back and say that nearly losing his legs must have made him a stronger candidate for world's fastest runner, contradictory as that seems.

How else can you explain an ordinary farm boy having the "something extra" that enabled him to outrun every sprinter on the planet?

Adversity makes us strong. If we don't give up, if we insist on taking life positively no matter what, we turn the sour into the sweet every single time. And patience is a power in itself.

SOLID CHARACTER

Paul says that patience leads to character.

Botanists tell us that there is a hidden function in the windiness of the month of March. We look outside and see the trees bending in the breeze, and we know those trees are being tested from the roots upward. But according to those who study such things, the gusts of wind help the trees flex their trunks and branches so that sap is drawn up through the center to nourish the limbs and budding leaves.

That is the effect that adversity can have upon us. We need to be shaken a little bit every now and then. It gets our juices flowing. And when we learn to bend, we have developed solid character. That word derives from the Greek word *charakter*, which once described the mark impressed upon a coin. You could say that the coin only became currency with value when the image of the ruler was painfully, through great heat and pressure, stamped upon it.

When we use the word today, we are talking about moral qualities. A man or woman of character has integrity and honesty. This person has a moral clarity that has been achieved by fighting through tough situations. If you have true character, the image of God has been stamped indelibly upon you through the unbearable heat and intense pressure of life—you are now his currency in this world. You have become a person of value, reflecting his image.

Helen Keller was blind and deaf very early in her life, completely isolated from any communication with the world. She knew what it meant to struggle, and she said, "Character cannot be developed in ease and quiet. Only through experience of trial and suffering can the soul be strengthened, ambition inspired, and success achieved."

Dave Dravecky is a true hero. A great pitcher in baseball, Dravecky was a National League All-Star with the San Francisco Giants and San Diego Padres and pitched in the World Series. In 1988 a cancerous tumor was found in his pitching arm. Following his surgery, he made a decision not to give up. He started his comeback the next season in the minor leagues, made it all the way back to the majors, and was pitching well in his comeback game when he reinjured his arm.

Dravecky tried two more comebacks, but eventually his arm and shoulder had to be amputated. Out of his experiences he wrote two books. The first, called *Comeback*, is the dramatic story of working to triumph over adversity. But his second book is called *When You Can't Come Back*, and it is by far the more profound and bittersweet of the two.

There are forms of adversity that simply cannot be overcome. Dave Dravecky knew he would never pitch another baseball game. But God had a new and amazing road for him to travel. As a devout believer in Jesus Christ, Dravecky devoted himself to building an organization, Outreach of Hope, to minister to people suffering from cancer or living with amputation. His impact on the world is vastly greater than it ever was when he stood on a small hill and threw a baseball.

Dravecky told two stories. The first was about the power of the human body and determination. The second, however, was a story of character in the face of adversity. The pitcher understood that God gives when life takes away.

Character is the sum of qualities that define who you really are. It guides your actions in moments of decision. Adversity builds it in so many ways when we encounter that adversity with the right attitude. Dravecky, for example, could have become bitter and angry. He could have shaken his fist at heaven; instead, he asked heaven for the next step.

A good example of the effect on character is found in our armed forces. How is training done in the military? Through adversity and plenty of it! Boot camp provides the wind that shakes a young tree down to its very roots and causes the sap to flow in healthy ways. It is a grueling and life-changing experience, and it molds strong men and women.

Young people come out of the military with life habits that serve them well all their lives. They understand what personal discipline is—quite a lesson for young people these days. They know the joy that comes through service to a cause. They grasp the concept of camaraderie through working in a group and watching one another's backs. They know all about actions and consequences. In most cases the adversity of military service builds true character.

ABOUNDING HOPE

The most surprising fruit of adversity is hope, yet Paul has already told us that patience produces character, and character produces hope.

I could tell you countless stories of people who *have it all*—wealth, power, fame, and the rest—yet possess cynical spirits. Then I could talk about so many people who have experienced far more than their share of adversity yet have felt the light of God shining through them in inverse proportion.

I have chosen one story to give you the idea. Fanny Crosby, much like Helen Keller, was stricken with blindness in childhood. At six weeks old she caught a simple cold that led to inflammation of the eyes. Then it so happened that the family doctor wasn't available, so a doctor with questionable credentials was called. He recommended that mustard plasters be placed on the eyes, and this was what brought on Fanny's blindness.

When she was only a year old, her father died. She was raised by her mother and grandmother. These two wonderful women raised Fanny Crosby with a strong spiritual faith, helping her to memorize thousands of verses from Scripture. For several years she attended a school for the blind and then became a teacher there. During this time she began to write poetry and experienced great success at it. She had a way with words.

The poetry, in turn, led to a career as one of the most famous and prolific hymn writers in church history. Though she didn't start writing the words for hymns until she was in her forties, Fanny Crosby wrote an incredible eight thousand hymns; she professed to spend time in prayer before writing every single one of them. She was also an impressive speaker in church.

She wrote so many excellent songs that she had to use pen names. The publishers of hymnals didn't want to give the impression that one person wrote most of the hymns, so her work would appear under multiple names. Lyrics about the goodness of God just flowed from her as if she were a fountain filled with living water. If you have ever sung "Blessed Assurance," "Jesus Is Tenderly Calling," "Praise Him, Praise Him," or "To God Be the Glory," you have sung a Fanny Crosby hymn.

She had the spiritual wisdom of someone who had to fight to lead a normal life. She saw her affliction as an opportunity for serving God, and she learned to speak spiritual truths in a musical language that would bless millions of people. Suffering has a way of humbling us, and humility has a way of opening us up to the truth. I tend to think that the adversity that poured into Fanny Crosby's life had a strong correlation with the wisdom that poured out, don't you? As in Glenn Cunningham's life, the furnace must have something to do with the strength of the steel that came out of it.

Not only was Fanny Crosby wise, but her affliction caused people to listen when she spoke about having joy or considering herself blessed. *If she can have so much power in a life spent in darkness*, they would think, *then there's nothing about my situation that says I can't too.*

She could say words not only beautifully but *credibly* simply because of her testimony of struggle. Here is an example:

All the way my Savior leads me; what have I to ask beside?
Can I doubt His tender mercy, who through life has been my Guide?
Heavenly peace, divinest comfort, here by faith in Him to dwell!
For I know whatever befall me, Jesus doeth all things well.
All the way my Savior leads me, cheers each winding path I tread,
Gives me grace for every trial, feeds me with the living bread.
Though my weary steps may falter, and my soul athirst may be,
Gushing from the Rock before me, lo! a spring of joy I see.[3]

You couldn't look at Fanny Crosby, knowing she could not look back, and doubt that she meant every word. I can't imagine living a single day without the use of my eyes, yet she has gone before me to show that in Christ all things are possible. Walking through adversity with God builds hope like nothing else in life.

I began this chapter by talking about the special joy of channeling our adversity into blessing by sharing it with others. Dave Dravecky did it. Fanny Crosby did it. To my great shock I found out that even I could help a man on the verge of suicide thousands of miles away.

God wants us to give him what we have even when it is not much, even when it is nothing but pain. He will take whatever we place in his hands and multiply it to minister to people we don't even know. In that way your pain becomes God's power base.

The greatest joy of my life these days is to help people through sharing my life experiences, as foolish as many of those experiences seemed at the time. When we stumble and fall and that becomes a channel of blessing for someone else, well, that's a miracle I will never take for granted.

I hope you will see your own struggles in a new way. They are there because God loves you, and they are the proof that daybreak always lies just beyond this present darkness. Invest your adversity wisely.

10
·······

Compassion:
Practice Radical Mercy

It doesn't matter who you are or what you are trying to accomplish in life; eventually you will have to deal with a difficult person—someone who either gets in your way or in some way opposes you. You can get fed up with these petty troublemakers and sell your house and move to another community, but you will find people there who are just as difficult. You can quit your job, give away all your possessions, and become a monk with a vow of silence in an out-of-the-way monastery, but before twenty-four hours have gone by, one of the other monks will probably be causing you problems. I suppose you could find a desolate, deserted island and move there, but I haven't tried that one. Let me suggest another option: try getting along with people.

Of course, you already know that it is not easy. Mark it up to human nature—to use Christian terminology, we're *fallen*. That means we are prone to pride and rebellion, two sins that tend to cause trouble whenever two or more people are gathered. It starts the moment we escape the cradle. Put two toddlers together, and they will start fighting over a toy. In elementary school we choose sides and create factions on the playground. Through the rest of life the most peaceable among us seem to have adversaries.

How much energy do we expend in trying to outmaneuver each other? How much time is wasted in petty squabbles? How many years do we take off our own lives by brooding over the little resentments that grow into lifelong obsessions? You and I have seen extended families destroyed by feuding and squabbling over the most ridiculous matters. Church meeting rooms often become battle zones, and our governmental bodies are characterized by internal warfare that stops progress in its tracks.

Until Christ comes again, that's just the way this world is going to be. But nobody said *you personally* have to live that way. Why not try a program of radical mercy and compassion?

The New Testament holds out a standard of making peace with everyone, including enemies and persecutors. Paul wrote, "Therefore let us pursue the things which make for peace and the things by which one may edify another" (Romans 14:19). Another passage says, "Pursue peace with all people, and holiness, without which no one will see the Lord" (Hebrews 12:14).

Then we are told, "Remind them to be subject to rulers and authorities, to obey, to be ready for every good work, to speak evil of no one, to be peaceable, gentle, showing all humility to all men" (Titus 3:1–2). It is very clear what the Bible is telling us. We are here to be peacemakers, not warmongers. It is a great shame that the world looks upon us and sees people who are angry and judgmental because that is precisely the condition for which we are to provide an alternative.

Jesus tells us to pray for our enemies. Every writer in the New Testament affirms the principle that we are to love not just those who are easy for us to love but the hard cases as well. I am going to show you that we should do this, first because it is right, second, because it is liberating and refreshing, and third, because it is a power base for leading a successful life.

In short I am going to show you a radical way of approaching difficult people: the way of compassion. It goes completely against the grain of human nature. It will make people look at you as if you are crazy. And it may well be the most powerful change you ever make in your life, short of becoming a child of God.

MISSING PUZZLE PIECES

In my first book I wrote a great deal about my father, who was the most profound influence on my life. I told how he gave me boxing gloves when I was young and taught me to be the same kind of warrior that he had always been. We spent time boxing, and I mean hard-hitting, knockdown boxing. My mom hated it, but Dad was determined to toughen me up. As it turned out, he did that job only too well.

His first rule for me had been, "Never start a fight. If you do, and I hear about it, you'll get a whipping at home."

Rule two was, "If someone starts a fight with you, and you don't fight back, you'll get a whipping when you get home."

Rule three was, "If I hear about you getting a whipping, you'll get another whipping when you get home."

The rules were nice and clear. I could not start a fight, but I could sure finish the ones that got started for me—and I'd better come out on top.

Daddy and I actually got along great even if I never felt I could measure up to his expectations. I grew up trying to emulate him, and in doing so I became a constant fighter. Don't get me wrong. I had a lot of fun during those growing-up years. I was a very likable and popular guy and tried to do the right thing as I had been taught. Still, I fought other people. I fought myself, and of course, I was fighting my mixed feelings about my dad. I never had a doubt that he loved me, but what I really wanted was his full approval.

When I got into one fight too many in college and was kicked out, I called my dad to come pick me up. He began chewing me out for being stupid enough to get into a fight. Finally I interrupted him. "Daddy," I said, "I'm exactly what you made me."

And he couldn't argue with that. We never talked about that fight again.

I moved along in life and found a career, but my confused feelings about my father were always with me. For one thing, as I became a follower of Jesus Christ, I wished my parents could have told me more about God. I realized they were good and loving parents, but I regretted not growing up in a more spiritually committed household.

That's why my own highlight of that first book was the way I found out, after my father's death, that he had indeed become a Christian. I had worried so much about the state of his soul and had experienced a profound sense of peace with this news. I realized that God has his own ways of reaching people. In time I had come to terms with the unfinished business in my relationship with the warrior who raised me to be a warrior.

When the book was released, I sent a copy to my dad's brother, Terrell, my last living uncle. After he read it, he told me that he had enjoyed it, but he felt I had painted my father in an overly harsh light.

I hated to hear that, of course. "I understand how the truth can be painful," I said, "but the thing is, I didn't share anything but facts."

He said, "Yes, of course, as far as you knew. But you never saw the whole picture. There are things about your dad you *don't* know. The two of us were close, you know, and we had secrets that we shared only with each other."

I caught my breath and said, "Can you give me an example?"

He said, "I believe so."

And he began to tell me an incredible, formative episode from the life of my father—one that my dad had never shared with me. Uncle Terrell was right. Just when I felt I had come to terms with my dad and my feelings about him, I was able to see him in a brand-new light.

THE STORY I'D MISSED

As I grew up, I was fascinated with the fact that my dad had fought in World War II. I pumped him for stories all the time, but he was highly reluctant to share them. So many men from his generation were like that when they returned from the awful realities of combat. They had witnessed horrible things when so many of them were right out of high school. As Stephen Ambrose has said, they were throwing hand grenades when they could have been throwing baseballs. They were proud to serve their country, but they wanted to move on with their lives without looking back and reliving painful memories.

Dad was in Europe in 1944 and '45. He fought through the hedgerows of France into Belgium, and he was at the Battle of the Bulge during that final frigid Christmas of the war, when the Germans made their last desperate push. It was a terrible, cold vigil along the front lines for the soldiers. They dug trenches, kept watch through the night, and simply tried to avoid frostbite. Eventually my dad was shipped home because his legs were frozen.

Before that happened, however, he was there when many of the Germans were coming forward and surrendering, particularly the older soldiers. These prisoners presented a logistical problem for the Allies. Our army was preparing to move out, to push across into Germany itself, and couldn't take the prisoners with them. Nor could they spare men to take them back behind the lines to prison camps. They certainly couldn't leave surrendering enemy soldiers alone because they would just have to fight them later. In many cases, therefore, there was one terrible solution to the problem, and it was prone to happen on both sides.

A German soldier came forward one day, hands in the air, holding his rifle over his head. He called out in German that he was surrendering and that he didn't want to be shot.

My dad's officer, a first lieutenant, took the rifle and pushed the prisoner toward Dad. He said, "Flynt, see that trail that leads back behind those trees? March this guy back there and shoot him."

My dad hesitated. He couldn't really see himself doing that. But the officer lit into dad and ordered him to go down that trail and take care of business.

Dad pushed his rifle barrel into the man's back and pointed toward the trail. The soldier just looked at him; he had indicated that he spoke no English. The two of them walked back behind the trees until they were out of sight. Dad gestured for the man to turn around, and then he cocked his rifle. The German, of course, knew exactly what was coming. His eyes met my dad's; four terrified eyes peered at each other in that moment of destiny.

Dad turned the man around again and marched him back where they had come from. He found the first lieutenant and said, "Sir, I just can't do it. I can't murder this man. If we are fighting, and he is trying to kill me, that's different. But I can't murder him, sir."

The officer cursed at him pretty severely, took his own rifle, and shoved the prisoner back down the trail yet again. A moment later two gunshots echoed through the trees. The prisoner was dead.

My dad felt as if he had failed. Maybe he felt he wasn't enough of a man, a strong enough warrior. But the next morning, the soldiers in Dad's unit came out of their foxholes and pushed forward on the attack. The first American casualty was the first lieutenant, the very one who had executed the prisoner on the previous day. He took a round right in the face and was dead on the spot.

For my dad, the two incidents were inextricably linked; that was the only way he could possibly see it. "If I had shot that German," he told my uncle, "that would have been me the next day. I'm convinced of that."

Uncle Terrell told me this story and repeated, "There were so many things your dad never shared with you."

THE STORY I KNEW

My uncle's story alone caused me to reassess a lot of things. It spoke to my dad's drive to make me tough, to make me a warrior, though I am certain he would have wanted me to make the same decision he did when ordered to kill in cold blood. The story spoke to his views of God and eternal justice, in that he believed he received cosmic mercy because he gave earthly mercy. I don't believe God was taking battlefield lives on that basis; life is a little more complex. But my dad believed it, and the incident made a tremendous impact on who he was.

I can even see why his complex emotions about the incident kept him from telling me about it even though I was pumping him all the time for war experiences. I can remember asking him, "Daddy, did you ever kill anybody? I don't mean along the firing lines, where everyone's shooting and nobody knows who shot who. I mean did you ever look one guy dead in the eye and then take his life?"

He would always make some dismissive comment and move on, but finally he gave in and told me what I wanted to know. Immediately I wished I could take the question back.

"I killed a young soldier once," he said. "He was a boy, a German boy, about fifteen—a fifteen-year-old SS officer. He was about the age your uncle Terrell was back then. I was twenty, and I had to kill him because he was coming at me.

So here I was, a twenty-year-old pulling the trigger on a fifteen-year-old who reminded me of my little brother."

He said, "Mike, I regret that I had to do that. There isn't a day that goes by that I don't think about that kid."

We were sitting on the patio at home when he finally told me that story, and I could see the remorse in his eyes, in his face, in his voice. I felt about one inch tall. I wanted to disappear into the concrete for tugging that story out of him.

But that was the story I knew. I had seen the warrior in him, forced to be cold-blooded by the need of the time—a kid barely out of his teens, made to shoot a kid barely out of puberty. The world does strange things to people.

What I didn't have was the other piece of the puzzle—I was missing at *least* one other piece, and how many more? I'm convinced that one of the greatest reasons Jesus told us not to judge others is that we lack too much information. If we had all the data on one another, surely we would see each other more sympathetically, right? We spend a great deal of time working up a good anger over people when, if we could go back and walk beside them on the path that brought them here, we would see them in an entirely different light.

I'm not saying that difficult people don't have free will or that they are not responsible for the wrong things they do. What I am saying is that they are part of a very flawed world that leaves its imprint on every one of us. We are fellow travelers, battling many of the same personal demons. Therefore, the first reason we must be compassionate is that we lack the understanding of who others are and what path they have walked.

Second, we must be compassionate because we lack the understanding of who *we* are. Jesus told a story that explains this concept beautifully.

MERCIFUL HEAVENS!

Matthew 18 tells about an occasion when Peter asked Jesus about the credit limit on forgiveness. How many times should he extend official forgiveness to one offender?

I get the idea Peter considered himself to be ahead of the curve on this one because he provided his own answer as he asked the question. He suggested *seven* as a good workable forgiveness limit. Don't laugh just because you know how Jesus answered it; for Peter (and probably for most of us), seven full forgiveness credits would actually have been a pretty impressive range of mercy. Some of us won't forgive someone *once*.

Jesus told Peter that the answer was more like "seventy times seven." I can just see Peter widening his eyes, then frantically counting his fingers and trying to do the math, but the point is actually not the mathematical figure. What Jesus was getting at was that the answer was closer to *exponential*. He was suggesting an unlimited credit line on forgiveness.

Well, that answer would have made no sense to the disciples at face value. Are we supposed to be doormats? Jesus, as always, told a story to make everyone see the issue from a whole new direction.

His parable went like this: There was a man who ran up a huge financial tab. I don't know how he spent it, whether he put it on a Samaritan Express credit card or what. He was ten thousand talents in the hole, but don't bother to convert that figure to modern dollars. Jesus' listeners had no money at all, and ten thousand meant about the same as a gazillion as far as they were concerned. Basically, this was one fellow who owed the national debt—to no less than the king. There was no payment plan in the world that was going to help him.

The king finally had the debtor brought in and said, "Well? Cash or check?"

The man knelt at the king's feet and pled his case. "Just a little more time," he said. "I'll pay every penny. Have a little mercy!" The penalty for lack of payment was imprisonment. And he would be sitting in his cell for a long time, waiting for such a debt to somehow be paid. Basically, he would be there until they came to carry his body away.

For some reason the king felt compassion for this guy, and he told him he was going to tear up the statement of debt. "Go your way," he said. "I am canceling your debt."

Now that is an incredible write-off! The man had walked in owing a monster sum and walked out owing exactly nothing. Life behind bars for him was commuted to total freedom and a clean record.

What would your emotions be like if you were in that man's sandals?

Well, a funny thing happened on his way to the celebration. The former debtor ran into a man who owed him a few hundred bucks (one hundred denarii). The Bible tells us that the man who had just been so miraculously forgiven suddenly changed into a beast. He "laid hands on him and took him by the throat, saying, 'Pay me what you owe!'" (Matthew 18:28). He then stood there imperiously and witnessed a repeat of the performance he had recently given: begging for time and mercy. But he did not have the compassion that had been given to him; he coldly ordered the debtor to be locked up.

When the king found out, of course, he was outraged. He revoked the amnesty he had handed out, called back the man with the larger debt, and put him in jail after all.

The point of the parable is this: if we walk around this planet withholding mercy, then we really do not understand who we are. Each one of us has accumulated a nearly infinite debt because we keep failing, on a nearly momentary basis, to live up to God's perfect standards. Our failure to be worthy of his love is staggeringly immense, exceeded only by the size of his mercy and forgiveness.

It is impossible to fully process what we have received and not be changed by it. If we continue keeping score of wrongs suffered, remembering every petty grievance, then something is terribly askew in our understanding of what we owe to God, who asks that we love one another with the love he has extended to us.

I am suggesting in this chapter that radical compassion and mercy are power bases for your life. Nothing holds us back more than the failure to get along with other people. Let's look at the key to extending mercy, then explore three powerful incentives for this policy as a life philosophy.

METHOD: GET THE WHOLE STORY

In his book *The 7 Habits of Highly Effective People*, Stephen Covey wrote about an experience he had on a subway train in New York City. It was a quiet, Sunday-morning ride during which the passengers were keeping to themselves, either reading, napping, or silently reflecting.

The train came to one of its stops, and a man and several children climbed aboard. The raucous children totally broke the silence, shouting, whining, crying, and playing. All the other passengers were clearly annoyed.

The man slumped down into the seat beside Covey. He seemed to be one of those parents who had developed immunity not only to his own children's behavior but also to the degree that they bother strangers. Covey watched as the children collided with surprised passengers, grabbed newspapers away, and continued their disruptive behavior. Covey was incredulous that the man never intervened. Really, enough was enough. He finally turned to the man and said, "Sir, your children are really disturbing a lot of people. I wonder if you couldn't control them a little more?"

The man seemed to come out of a trance as he said, "Oh, you're right. I guess I should do something about it. We just came from the hospital where their mother died about an hour ago. I don't know what to think, and I guess they don't know how to handle it either."

Covey felt something like I did when I was sitting on that patio, insisting that my dad answer a difficult question. Covey felt very small too. He told this story as an example of a paradigm shift. It is like one of those pictures that when viewed one way is a dark vase and when viewed another way is two light faces, peering at one another in front of a dark background.

The whole picture can change in an instant. When we have all the facts, our emotions are transformed. We begin to think differently. Covey's irritation was washed away, and compassion flowed in to take its place. Soon he was offering comfort and asking what he could do to help.

I grew up in the same house as my father, but I still lacked information about central events in his background. Covey made a quick judgment about a fellow passenger, and he found out how inappropriate that judgment was.

We are all fellow passengers on this ride of life. If we are going to reach our goals, we need to learn how to stop getting in each other's way; rather than wasting our precious energy on conflict and accepting an obvious negative judgment as the final analysis, we need to focus on finding the positives in every situation. We need to get the whole story on one another. No, I am not suggesting you put a private detective on retainer, but I think we can all afford to assume that if someone takes actions that bother us, there is some extenuating circumstance that, if we only knew about it, would tend to enhance our compassion.

Even if somehow there is *no* reason for someone's poor behavior—that is, this guy was just born ornery and cantankerous, period—God gives us no option for maintaining an enemy list. As we have seen, he refuses to put us on his own enemy list. We all use the same measure of God's mercy, and we all must extend it. There are no good guys or bad guys here, just forgiven sinners.

Incidentally, God will help you with this little project. I know of one prayer he has answered in my life every single time I have prayed it: "Lord, give me *your* love for this person." When you feel you can't love someone from your own perspective, God has all the stuff you need. He will fill your heart with compassion if you simply ask him to do it. It feels great to let go of resentment.

Let's look at the benefits of traveling through life without bitterness toward others.

BENEFIT: TRAVELING LIGHT

The most dangerous element of bitterness is that its victims never realize its power over them. Recently a famous NFL wide receiver was elected to the Pro Football Hall of Fame. We won't use his name here, but we will describe his bitterness. He felt that it had taken far too many years for him to receive this prestigious honor and that this was the fault of the quarterback who threw passes to him. As he was inducted into the Hall, he made a big point of blaming the quarterback (who had four Super Bowl rings, by the way).

That quarterback heard these comments, of course. He said that what really struck him was that on such a happy day of celebration, a man could be consumed by thoughts of resentment. I am sure the receiver had not thought about that. Bitterness does that to us.

I heard about a Bible study leader who did a brilliant job explaining what it means to unburden ourselves from bitterness. He instructed each group member to bring a clear plastic bag and a sack of potatoes to the weekly meeting. Then he said, "Let's do this exercise together. Write down the name of every person you have a grudge against. Write each name on one potato, along with the date. Then put all those potatoes in the plastic bag you brought."

The leader then told the members to take the plastic bag everywhere they went. As you can imagine, they began to look at each other in disbelief at this point. "Put the bag beside your bed at night," said the leader. "Have it there beside you on the car seat while you drive, on your desk at work, and in your lap as you watch television at night."

A couple of the members actually tried it. Their bags were heavy. Dragging all those potatoes around and keeping an eye on them was no fun from the beginning. But when the potatoes began to become moldy and putrid and began to sprout eyes, the point became more than clear. When we forgive, we are the primary beneficiaries. When we carry our bitterness around, it is an irrational self-punishment. We are the ones who must carry the load.

BENEFIT: TRAVELING COMPANIONS

The second benefit of mercy is that it allows us to travel farther. Enemies keep us away from our goals in two ways. First, they may actively work against us, and second, they sap our emotional energy. We spend precious time either struggling with people or worrying about them. Think about how much anxiety in your life is caused by poor relationships—people at the office who get under your skin, folks in your neighborhood or at church. What would your life be like if you could be free of the human skirmishes that become such distractions?

Hey, I'm not saying it's easy. It may be one of the single most difficult things to do in life, and it is also true that you will never do it perfectly. There are simply some people who are angry enough or damaged enough that they will continue to cause problems no matter what. But you can make a radical difference in your life just by converting a few to friends and forgiving the rest without condition.

This principle—enemies to friends—was the make-or-break issue of the early church. Christianity began as a Jewish sect, and soon non-Jews (Gentiles) wanted to be a part of it. There was plenty of apprehension on both sides, but Paul was determined to see people with conflicting views of life become friends. He wrote:

> Christ himself is our peace. He made both Jewish people and those who are not Jews one people. They were separated as if there were a wall between them, but Christ broke down that wall of hate by giving his own body . . . His purpose was to make the two groups of people become one new people in him and in this way make peace. It was also Christ's purpose to end the hatred between the two groups, to make them into one body, and to bring them back to God. Christ did all this with his death on the cross. (Ephesians 2:14–16 NCV)

Jesus said, "But I say to you who are listening, love your enemies. Do good to those who hate you" (Luke 6:27 NCV). This is what separates us from everyone else. If we as Christians have the same bitterness as everyone else, exactly what is there about us that makes God look good? Why would anyone look at us and want to be a part of our faith?

In 1818, Christian missionaries succeeded in converting Tamatoe, an emperor on one of the islands of the South Pacific. His people were not too pleased about the news, and a plot quickly developed. The conspirators were going to seize Tamatoe and the other new believers, take them away, and burn them to death on an open fire in the name of their own pagan gods.

But Tamatoe, a wily leader, beat them at their own game. Before they could seize him, he seized them. Of course, they expected a quick execution instead of what actually happened. They were taken back to the palace, where a great feast was laid before them. The plotters were astounded by the idea of hospitality and goodwill extended by a murder target. They began to ask questions about what could have changed Tamatoe so much, about what this strange new God was all about. Before the night was over, they burned their idols and became Christians. Life just works better when we cut our losses and bury the hatchet—and I don't mean in someone's back!

As you pursue your goals in life, I challenge you to keep an enemy list—and consider it a prayer list. Do exactly what Jesus said and pray every single day for people with whom you struggle. You simply won't find it possible to keep resenting individuals for whom you are sincerely praying. God will start showing you those people as he sees them. Ask him to do something extraordinary and help you create alliances with at least some so that everyone is working for common goals rather than the goal of making each other miserable.

BENEFIT: TRAVELING MERCIES

Finally, there is the principle that we experience the greatest joys and the deepest awareness of God when we make peace with one another. Since Christ came to make peace between God and humanity and among people themselves, we are fully aligned with his purposes when we knock down those dividing walls and create unity where there is hostility.

Have you ever witnessed a moment of powerful reconciliation? A parent and child making up after a fight, bickering business partners reunifying, or feuding branches of a family embracing in mutual forgiveness? There is something genuinely holy about an occasion when people humble themselves, put aside their prejudices and resentments, and become friends. This is when we know we are created in the image of God. Humility and the swallowing of pride are not ordinary products of human nature.

Corrie ten Boom was the author of the classic book *The Hiding Place*, which recounted her experiences during World War II in a German prison camp. Her sister and father died in similar camps, and she herself survived only after bitter hardship. But she never doubted God's goodness, no matter what new humiliations and degradations occurred. For example, the women were forced into showers to control the lice, and male German guards would watch them, ridicule them, and make lewd remarks.

Corrie made it a firm discipline of her life to forgive everyone, regardless of the gravity of their offense. The cruel, sometimes murderous prison guards were on that list, and she felt she had fully forgiven them in Christ's power.

After the war she traveled throughout Europe and the United States, speaking in churches and at gatherings, sharing her experiences. One Sunday she found herself sharing her experiences with a congregation in Munich. After church a man stepped up to introduce himself. He put out his hand and said, "*Ja, Fräulein*, it is wonderful that Jesus forgives us all our sins, just as you say."

She immediately recognized the face. This was an SS guard who had stood at the shower stall and humiliated her along with countless other women. For a moment she could not lift her hand to meet his. Surely God would not expect that from her after all this man had done, right?

But she remembered her prayer list. Hadn't she told herself this guard was forgiven? Are there loopholes in forgiveness? Are there limits? Or must it be absolute?

God's love, she reflected, was infinite and unconditional. And that is what he expects from us. This man, once a demon from hell in her view, now stood before her as a supreme test of the reality of her commitment to Christ. Instantly and silently she prayed, "Lord, forgive me, I cannot forgive."

Even as the words poured from the depth of her soul, she felt God's forgiveness and full mercy for her offense of standing before the world to accept plaudits for being a world-class forgiver when she wasn't one at all. Her hand came unstuck, the hatred dispersed like so much dust in a strong breeze, and she took the man's hand.

Corrie ten Boom had done what the man in the parable could not. She had fully accepted God's mercy, and that allowed her to fully extend it.

If you are like many of us, there are people on your list whom you cannot forgive. They may have done much less than a German SS guard in a concentration camp; nonetheless, there it is: you cannot forgive them. I would invite you *not* to beat yourself up about that. Human nature being what it is, we all end up carrying the emotional residue of interpersonal clashes. To err (or have ire) is human; to forgive, divine.

And that is the whole point. It is in your nature to be angry, for we are children of wrath. It is in God's nature to be abounding with unconditional, incomprehensible, and boundless love. If you are running just a bit low on mercy, why not borrow some from God? That is the ultimate source of every drop of it anyway.

One Friday afternoon as the sky darkened, Jesus hung on a cross with nails through his hands and feet, thorns pricking his brow, and the last of his breath laboring from his lungs. His body was bruised all over, and his spirit was wounded by the sheer vengefulness of the public that had turned against him—the public he had touched, taught, healed.

As he prepared to give himself over to death, he shouted out no recriminations, no threats of eternal vengeance from God or his squadrons of angels. Instead, he did precisely the opposite thing—the least intuitive thing imaginable from a human perspective.

He made an alliance with the same human race that had tortured and crucified him. First, he said, "Father, forgive them, for they do not know what they do" (Luke 23:34). Then he went before the Father and exchanged his perfection, his righteousness, for the sins of the whole world so there could be mercy on every sinner who ever lived.

Please realize that he did this proactively. Nobody asked him to go to that cross or to give up his heavenly place to wear flesh and sustain all our abuse. Somehow he loved us, even knowing every single flaw in our collective character. And if you had been the only human being who ever lived, he would have done it all for you in just the same way. That was how he demonstrated his love, his compassion, his mercy.

Now, can you tell me what that other person did to make you so angry? Can you tell me how unthinkable his or her crime was and that forgiveness is out of the question?

When you learn the life discipline of cultivating friends and absolutely refusing to collect enemies—when you make it a point to reach out to those who have wronged you, and *serve* them—you will have discovered a power base that may be the most miraculous, dynamic, and supernatural of all. You will be living according to the blueprint that God has devised for each of us. And, my friend, you will begin to change the world. Radical mercy is just that powerful.

Who is the first person on your list?

11

Time: Maximize Your Moments

Our family living room is a formal and tidy place—it is a fine room, but we reserve it for special occasions. It does not have that cozy feel of our den or kitchen. And late one particular evening when the rest of my family had gone to bed, it was a lonely place.

The year was 1988, and it was the last night of August. I sat forward, my head resting in my hands, and I wondered what kind of future I could hope for.

I reached over to the thin sheet of paper and studied it yet again, as if that would change anything. It was a lab report from Dr. Andrews's office—my blood work. This day had brought the worst-case scenario that we spend our lives dreading. We tell ourselves it will never come and go about our business. Until it comes.

Dear God—how can this be?

Several weeks earlier life was blissfully humdrum and uneventful with no doctors' voices to be heard. But I wasn't sleeping well. During the middle of each night, I would awaken with a feeling of dread. At first I attributed it to some big issues in my business ventures. A lot was going on there. But on second thought I knew better than that. This was coming from my body. It was trying to tell me something, giving me a little nudge and an inaudible whisper that said, *You better look inside here*. It also said, *Go and get a checkup—do it now*.

How many years had it been since I had a full physical? Gosh, I didn't even want to think about that. I was one of those people who came from good stock, who simply refused to be sick. I never missed work, never caught a cold or the flu, and never had a fever. I had not been sick since I was twelve years old. It was a point of pride. Sickness was not for guys like me.

Eileen has always said that I have an outstanding immune system; I have never been sick in the thirty-eight years she has known me. I feel that not having a negative attitude about getting sick has something to do with my remarkable record. I just take a positive approach to sickness and believe that I am not going to get sick, and I don't. In 1988, she had known me for seventeen years without having to put me in bed and bring me chicken soup.

So why was I waking up in the middle of the night with a feeling of mortal anxiety? *All those years without a physical,* came the whisper. *Anything could be growing inside you, building up strength. You could even have . . .*

Once those things came into my mind, sleep was out of the question. I prayed, I quoted every Scripture verse I knew, I took mental inventory of every muscle from my head to my feet but all to no avail. Nothing remained but to climb out of bed because tossing and turning would disturb my wife. I wasn't about to let her share my lack of rest with our third child due in a month.

I punted my pride issue and went to get a physical. Why not? I was likely to pass with flying colors; it would put an end to the midnight jitters.

So I went, and the physical seemed to be a success. The doctor anticipated no problems whatsoever. Then the next day the bottom fell out. He called me back to his office and placed in my hands a sheet with a line that read, in all caps:

MANY DEGENERATIVE CELLS ARE OBSERVED IN THIS SPECIMEN.

Dr. Andrews took more blood, hesitant to tell me much about the implications of the phrase *degenerative cells*. He mentioned leukemia, and he mentioned the need for me to avoid overreacting. The lab was standing by, waiting for more samples.

I don't tend to watch shot needles closely, but I did this time because my mind was far away. How was I going to tell Eileen? Or was I going to tell her? No—I wasn't. At this stage of a pregnancy, she did not need any extra anxiety.

Late that night, alone in the living room, I looked up leukemia in a medical reference book. In the case of chronic leukemia, I noted three to five years might be my life expectancy.

I quietly returned that book to the shelf and picked up my Bible. I began reading in Psalms and Proverbs, flipping aimlessly through the pages. For some reason King Hezekiah came to my restless mind. I found his story of healing in 2 Kings 20:1–11, and I scanned the narrative with a new sense of urgency.

After a while I put the Bible down and sat quietly, then thought, *Is this what it's like to have your life flash before you?* I reviewed the years that passed so quickly and eventfully. Time is relentless. I thought of the crazy things I did before I knew Christ. It occured to me that it's a wonder I had made it alive that far. I smiled a little. But then I thought of my wife and children, particularly the one developing inside Eileen, and how much they needed me. I wondered about the hardship it would be on Eileen, watching me go through chemotherapy to fight a debilitating disease.

I slid to my knees and then fell on my face on the living room floor. I told God just what was in my heart. "Oh, Lord," I said, "if I've done anything, *anything*, to bring on this cancer in my blood, I'm sorry! But you have been so good to me. I could never complain in light of the multitude of blessings you have poured out on the life of a violent man."

The tears were flowing, and I followed the example of Hezekiah. I asked God to remember me as a good man—I have made more than my share of mistakes, but every one of them is covered by the blood of Jesus. All forgiven.

Then I began to plead with God, not for my own sake but for that of my family: my wife and my children need me. "Heal me of this disease," I said, weeping, "so that I can care for my family and continue serving you." Emotionally spent, I continued to lie on the floor for a few moments, thinking of Hezekiah and his healing. Then I went to bed and slept quite well.

TIME IN PERSPECTIVE

As I rose the next day, I realized that my outlook on time had forever changed. I didn't want to lie in bed an extra minute. There was a new sense of urgency.

Time is a little like a half-pound package of gourmet coffee. When you unwrap the coffee, that fragrant smell permeates the room. As you dig into the package, you get a nice, rounded scoop of the coffee so that your cup will be strong and hearty. You don't give a single thought to how much coffee is left, only to how good you want it to taste right then.

A few weeks later you find yourself coming to the bottom of that package. You measure your scoop carefully, not needing your cup to be quite so extravagantly strong. You want the bag to last, but it comes and goes too quickly.

I had thought about my life span in the past but not with any degree of anxiety. I was the captain of my fate, insofar as I could care for my body. I was confident I could be in the top percentile of fitness for whatever age and stage I might reach. I watched what I ate and drank; I had no bad habits. I used little things like walking up the steps as opportunities for extra exercise—I would take the steps two at a time, lifting my knees high to get the best muscular benefit—and I avoided elevators.

But the elevator of life brings you closer to the top floor every day. You can work out, you can run, but you cannot hide. At some point the elevator reaches the end of its journey. Most of us have some kind of warning as we approach our top floor. Then we see things differently. We measure each moment of life as something special. Oh, to have just one of those wasted days, weeks, or even months from the past again! What we would do with them now? How different our priorities would be. We might even stop and smell a few roses—if only we had the time. I am reminded of Tim McGraw's popular song "Live Like You Were Dying."

Eileen wanted to accompany me to the doctor's office the next day. For her it was a beautiful day, and she wanted to get out of the house. I did not share the previous day's lab report with her. I decided to just wait until I received the *final* word from Dr. Andrews and then pray about how and when I should break the news to Eileen.

Dr. Andrews's office was in the same building, right upstairs from my office. He had indicated that he would call me early with the results from the second round of testing. Eileen and I had just settled in at my office when the phone rang. I very nonchalantly answered it. My heart raced as Dr. Andrews's secretary informed me that he would like to speak with me right away if that was possible. I told her I would be right up.

I told Eileen it was Dr. Andrews, wanting to speak with me about the results from my physical, and I would be right back. As I walked up the stairs to his office, I was praying and trying to imagine how I was going to break this news to Eileen. For me that was the hardest part of this whole process, trying to see myself telling Eileen and our children that I had leukemia.

When I stepped into Dr. Andrews's reception area, he was standing there waiting for me and motioned for me to come into his office. Once again he had a sheet of paper sitting on his desk. My heart was pounding as he slowly slid it across his desk to where I was standing. His finger was on a statement right where the words *degenerative cells* had been the day before. Now, however, the message was changed:

NORMAL AND ADEQUATE.

I don't remember walking to his sofa, but that's where I was the next moment I can remember. I lost about ten seconds somewhere. What wonderful, beautiful words: *normal and adequate.* I never expected words to be so sweet.

To what could we attribute the change? The doctor had no answers. He had double-checked everything, and both samples—the degenerative ones and the normal ones—had come from the same patient. It defied the expectations of science. The doctor had a more philosophical explanation. He smiled and said, "I guess God is trying to show you how much he loves you."

It is hard to describe the tremendous relief and joy I felt as I walked back downstairs to my office. I tried to make sense of what had just happened. Had it been a mistake? No, Dr. Andrews said he had double-checked everything to make sure both samples had been my blood. And then I just kept thinking about his statement, "Maybe God is trying to show you how much he loves you." I was truly overwhelmed and humbled beyond words.

I sat down with Eileen and shared with her all that had taken place in the last forty-eight hours, from the initial lab report to the final results and the statement made by Dr. Andrews. She turned pale, hugged me, and said she was so grateful for the second set of results and God's mercy. We just sat and held each other for a long time. She told me she had no idea how I could keep something like that to myself. But she said, "You did the right thing. I know it was out of love and concern for me."

I smiled and asked, "Would you like to pray with me?"

We knelt together in my office and poured out praise and worship to our loving Father. My heart was so full, and so were my eyes. We dedicated ourselves to the lifelong service of such a gracious and merciful God.

And at that very moment I made a covenant with myself to hold close to my heart the treasure that I now understood I had all along—the precious gift called *time*.

TIME IN PERSPECTIVE

Time is entirely relative, isn't it? I heard a story that makes that point—although I admit it would not have amused me at all during my brief period of anxiety. There was a man just like me who went to the doctor to get his test results. The doctor told him he had some bad news and some worse news for him. Which did he want first?

The patient wasn't too pleased with his choices, but he said he would take the bad news first.

"You have twenty-four hours to live," said the doctor.

The patient went into a state of panic. "That's terrible!" he said. "Twenty-four hours? How can I possibly get my affairs in order by that time? And what in the world could be worse news?"

The doctor said, "The worse news is that I was supposed to tell you this yesterday."

The patient, you see, only *thought* he lacked time with the first piece of information. Now he found out he had no time at all. And as we all know (but are reluctant to admit), that's how life is. We really do not know how long we have. So how do we handle that fact?

Let's imagine someone takes you to a large building and says, "Somewhere in this building you will find one million dollars. You have a limited period of time to find it. But I am not going to tell you what that time period is—we will just lock all the doors and pull you out at the right time."

Do you think you would wander through the building looking for the money, taking your time, stopping for a cup of coffee every now and then? Not if you were smart. You would feel a sense of urgency about it. You could run out of time in five seconds or sooner, so you had better maximize every moment.

That is where we find ourselves in this world. I happen to believe this life is not the end. I will spend eternity with my Lord, and I will be reunited with all those I have lost who had a saving relationship with Jesus, including parents and friends. But that does not mean I don't have a lot to do in this life, here and now. The blood work incident helped me understand that at some point—I know not when—the doors will be locked, and I will be pulled out. Although I will go to a better place, I want to take care of business in this place first. In this chapter I hope I can give you some valuable and practical tips on how I do that and how you can too.

Our first perspective, then, is that our time is indefinite. Even if we have half a century left, we want to live every moment to its fullest and accomplish what God placed us here to do.

The second perspective to understand is that time is part of creation. That is, it is something God made, and he lives outside of it. That is hard for us to understand because we ourselves have never been *outside* of time. He sees past, present, and future simultaneously, though we live entirely in the single moment that is the present. The Bible tells us "that with the Lord one day is as a thousand years, and a thousand years as one day" (2 Peter 3:8).

It is important to remember that time is just one more thing God rules. He has a purpose for time, and he gives us exactly the time we need. The Bible contains many examples of God's use of time. We are told that he sent his Son in "the fullness of the time" (Galatians 4:4) and that in "the fullness of the times He might gather together in one all things in Christ, both which are in heaven and which are on earth—in Him" (Ephesians 1:10).

"The fullness of the time" is a phrase that tells us that God has a plan and a good schedule for carrying it out. We want to imitate him in that, using our time in the wisest possible way, living our lives to the fullest—full-time. We want to be "redeeming the time" (Colossians 4:5) while we have the daylight to do it.

Obviously, using time well is a matter of setting priorities. I am going to assume you know that already, and I will avoid wasting space giving you your hundredth lecture on the subject. We all know that we need to figure out what is most important to us and pursue that first while eliminating the things that are unworthy of our time. Check. Beyond that time-honored time tip, here are a few other practical ideas you can use.

SOW IN HEALTH, REAP IN TIME

You won't be the least bit surprised to hear this one from me, but here it is. Assuming you are going to live the ordinary life expectancy (currently seventy-seven to eighty years), the best thing you can do to increase the span of your life is to maximize your health. As someone who played college football at fifty-nine years old, I feel qualified to tell you that. But if you don't believe me, ask your doctor for the literature. It will show you just how many years you will forfeit by being a smoker, how many by drinking immoderately, how many for every ten pounds you weigh over the optimal weight range, and so on.

If you begin to eat right, get a reasonable amount of exercise, avoid bad habits, and keep a positive frame of mind, you are statistically more likely to live longer. This is the only possible way you can arrange for more time. Remember the parable about the rich fool in Luke 12? He amassed all his wealth and thought he could buy all that he wanted, but God took his life that very night. You can't buy time, but you can extend your lease by seeing to your health.

Of course, it's not just a matter of the quantity of years. Those golden years will be far more golden when you feel good physically. If you are carrying around extra weight or if you have done other things to damage your health, then you will feel fortunate to be alive, but you will watch some of your healthier friends with a good bit of envy. If you keep your body in good shape, you will be able to manage time from a much more positive mind-set.

I like being able to run every day in my early sixties. I enjoy having the ability to work out on my Powerbase (the fitness equipment I invented) the way I have for almost ten years now. After a good, vigorous day I sleep better than many people my age. My cells replenish themselves more effectively because I have maintained the "temple of the Holy Spirit" (1 Corinthians 6:19) that is the human body. Wouldn't you hate to walk into your church and see that it has been trashed, that garbage is all over the floors and the walls are falling in? Your body is the church where God comes to live, and it should be cared for with reverence.

If you will pardon my wording, here is food for thought. The *New England Journal of Medicine* tells us that the friends you favor have a great effect on the waistline you wear. The threat of obesity increases 57 percent if a person's friends are overweight. Maybe if you look around and see people as flabby as you, it is easier to justify staying away from the gym and the diet plan. Don't let your mind find ways to rationalize not staying in shape.

More about this one in the next chapter, but for now my point is this: what you sow in good health, you reap in extended, quality time on this planet.

MEASURE YOUR PROGRESS

Here is a quick index to tell you where you are in managing your time. It plays on a question political candidates often ask: Are you better off this year than you were a year ago?

That is, are you progressing toward your goals? Can you break down the various key elements of your life—work, family, spiritual life, other goals— and see how you have progressed?

Sure, the answer is discouraging for most of us. At New Year's, we are encouraged to make those lists of resolutions, and we do it knowing in our heart of hearts that we are not going to stick with it. Most people who routinely attend a gym have to fight for a parking place in January; then it gets a little easier in February, and by March the rush is over; resolutions have fallen through. We are not so bad at setting goals; the problem is in the follow-through.

I find it is very helpful not to let my goals hide inside my brain. I need to tell people about them so they can hold me accountable. I need to write them down on poster board and have a timeline for when I should accomplish each step that will lead me to my ultimate goal. I study my Bible every single day, but I know it won't happen if I don't manage my time and keep up. Each day there are plenty of reasons I could be doing something else, but I have ingrained it as a regular habit to keep on schedule, and I follow through.

The reason that can happen for me is that I have a well-measured plan. There is a schedule that I follow, and if I am obedient to that schedule, I know I will be studying God's Word 365 days a year. So why don't we do that with other things? Write down exactly what you would like to accomplish during the next month; then create a timeline for accomplishing that goal. This will give you measurable steps.

It is not always as easy as reading a set number of Bible verses or doing a specific number of push-ups or reps in the weight room. But there are ways to measure progress toward most goals. Our great mistake is in imagining that castle in the sky without conceptualizing the stairway we have to climb to get to it and each step it takes.

When it comes to time management, we believe we don't have time to get certain things done. That is nearly always a misconception. We believe this because we look at the faraway goal we would like to attain, and think, *That's huge! No way I have the time to achieve it.* I can tell you about football teams that have set up on their own twenty-yard line and made a touchdown much farther away than it needed to be, by trying to get it all in one big throw down the sidelines. The much better end-game strategy is to nickel-and-dime it down the field, getting a chunk here and a chunk there. The eighty yards seem to shrink when a team does that.

It is the same way with big goals. The best way to eat an elephant, they say, is one bite at a time. You would feel better about that goal if you viewed it in terms of little chunks. That is where strategy comes in.

Clear strategy makes time suddenly seem accessible—no matter what the goal is. I'll give you an example of a goal that is much more complex than reading or exercising. Your goal may be to earn a promotion at work.

First, I would comment that you may be setting a goal you can't be responsible for achieving. That is true if you rely on someone else, such as a supervisor, to promote you. True goals involve outcomes you can control. Dreams and visions are a little more flexible; you aim toward them in the long term, knowing you will need some help—from God and others—to finally get there. But goals should be clear, tangible, and within reach. They should also be realistic. (Trying to lose 150 pounds in a year may not be realistic, for example.)

Okay, so maybe it is more of a dream to get that job promotion. A goal would be a work objective you can plan: make fifty sales calls this month, contact twenty-five new clients, or volunteer for ten assignments that belong to coworkers to demonstrate a team attitude. You can't control all the factors that would lead to a promotion, but you can do everything in your power to earn it by setting attainable goals that will make your work shine. Then once you have written down those goals, you can mark your progress each day and see yourself move satisfactorily toward an exciting achievement. Nothing makes me feel better than making a small check mark sometimes. I always say about my workouts, "This was one thing I got done today that is tangible and healthy—no matter what else happens today."

Break the important tasks in your life down to measurable assignments. Once you do, you will be amazed at how much time you find to accomplish them. This bite-size approach leads us to our next insight.

AVOID THE TYRANNY OF THE URGENT

Charles E. Hummel wrote a classic booklet called *Tyranny of the Urgent*. He made an amazing observation about how we use time. We spend most of it, he said, doing nonessential things while the truly important ones go by the board. Why is that the case? Certain things, though they aren't as important in the long run, are made to seem urgent today.[1]

"Tyranny of the urgent" is really a more philosophical way of saying, "The squeaky wheel gets the grease." The other wheels, of course, are just as important, but we pay attention to the one we can hear. In everyday life it is the same way. How much time do we spend in *urgent* pursuits that are really not the ones that will lead us where we want to go?

Again, it is important to know exactly what dream you are pursuing. What is the great, overarching goal for your life, and what are the goals in the departments of family, career, your soul, and the rest? Once you know what those are and once you have followed our first step and defined how you are going to get there, one bite at a time, your daily agenda suddenly has a new layer of clarity. You look at certain scheduled or nonscheduled activities and say, "Gosh, that will take half my day yet will not help me progress toward the things that are most important to me."

I have exercise goals. I have goals for reading the Scriptures. These are clear and concrete, and I have them written into my daily schedule; therefore, I get them done. If your schedule is first-come-first-serve, you are going to make a lot less progress getting where you want to go. Believe me, the squeaky wheels of our lives will line up and be *first come* every time. The urgent will be more tyrannical than ever.

I am not recommending that you become a robot, giving time only to essential things. If that happened, a friend would call you in need of someone to talk to, and you would say, "Sorry, but that won't help me reach my goals." We need to be open to the surprises, the people, and the events that the Holy Spirit brings before us. Our daily planners are not carved in stone. However, if we have established which people, places, and things are the important ones, we will be empowered to make the little time decisions throughout the day that keep us from becoming sidetracked.

You might be able to make a few permanent changes that are helpful too. I took a good look at my schedule and quit golf because it consumed four hours that I would otherwise spend with my family. I tried to kill two birds with one stone by getting them interested in golf, but it didn't take. That forced me to make a decision about what was truly important to me, and my family won. Now, do I have regrets about the lost hours on the green? Truthfully, no. Have I gotten much more out of the increased time with my family? Absolutely. Your loved ones require quantity time *and* quality time, by the way.

The little time decisions will be the most difficult battles, however. You know the ones I mean. The classic solution bears repeating as well-known as it is—and it carries a classic story with it. You may have heard it already, but it won't hurt you to do so again. The best thing about it is that it is completely true.

Ivy Lee was a management consultant. Charles Schwab of Bethlehem Steel Company hired him to come in and help him manage his time. Lee said, "In the morning, write down the six most important things you have to do that day. Put them in order of importance. Start with number one."

Schwab listened, no more impressed than you are right now, and asked, "What's your fee for telling me that?"

Lee said, "That's up to you. Try it exactly as I gave it to you for several months. Then write me a check for what you think the advice was worth."

Several months later Ivy Lee received a check for twenty-five thousand dollars. By the way, this happened at the beginning of the twentieth century when that was an even larger sum of money than it is today.[2]

You see, this isn't rocket science. It is laser science because it is all about the intensity of your focus. If you know exactly what is essential and what isn't, you are on the right track. If you can prioritize the essential things, you are on your way. If you can drop the nonessentials down to the bottom of the list (even if you get yelled at by a few squeakers), you are nearly home. You won't believe how many goals you will start to reach and how much better your life will be.

MAKE TECHNOLOGY YOUR FRIEND, NOT YOUR ENEMY

Have you noticed that technology is always presented as the great solution to time management although it ends up consuming much more time than it saves? How many hours have you lost waiting for someone to come fix your computer?

It would be easier to make our peace with new technology if it would just stand still for a moment! A few years ago we got all our transactions switched from snail mail to e-mail, and then everyone started using cell phones. We got used to the cell phones, and then people started texting. I have no idea why typing words into a phone seems more efficient than simply speaking into it, but I just do as I am told. I do know that keeping up with technology becomes a huge time waster if we are not careful.

We really don't have the option of choosing not to participate. Computers and the Internet drive our economy, our social lives, and everything else these days. The key is to keep up but to keep our tech toys from disrupting the things that are most important. For example, if the operating system on your computer is working well, don't fix what isn't broken. As long as the manufacturer supports it and it doesn't become an obstacle to communication, stick with what you know. If we are going to procrastinate about something, let's procrastinate about adopting new technologies that have time-consuming learning curves. Those who make our phones and computers want us to keep upgrading and learning new systems, which, of course, brings in profits to their companies. Make only the changes that you are certain are going to help you get more done.

Meanwhile, do keep an ear to the ground for new technology that can help you. Communication never has been more effective. We can post a simple status update on a social networking service such as Facebook, and dozens of friends will have that information immediately. We can find people more quickly with these cell phones, as irritating a presence as they may be. And in this day and age, Web sites are a wonderful way for people to get many things done and to deliver different kinds of information.

Pastors I know use Bible software that holds any number of Bible translations, all kinds of commentaries, and all the other reference books they need. Rather than spending hours looking things up and finding the right pages in the right books as they prepare their sermons, they can pull up all the right information on a computer with a couple clicks of the mouse. Technology, then, is not evil. We simply need to make it our friend and use all the right programs and devices to cut out the interruptions that keep us from getting more done. You do know your cell phone has an Off button and voice mail, don't you?

FILL IN THE BLANKS

Time comes in all sizes. Did you know that?

Charles Spurgeon once took a large mason jar and asked an audience, "How many of these billiard balls do you think will fit in here?" People made guesses, and then he dropped the balls in until they filled the jar. "Is the jar full?" he asked. Everyone agreed it was.

"I disagree," said Spurgeon, producing a big bag of marbles. "Who thinks I can get some of these in there?" All hands were raised again, and guesses were made on how many might fit. Spurgeon was able to get a good number of the marbles into the jar. "Is it full yet?"

No one was certain, so Spurgeon produced a can of dirt. He dumped it into the jar until it came to the rim. That had to be the limit—now everyone agreed the jar was full.

Not yet. Spurgeon showed everyone a pitcher of water, and yes, a good bit of it went into that mason jar without spilling.

"I think it's full," he said.[3]

Time comes in all sizes. It has more blank spaces than you think it does. We also start out with the billiard balls, the big tasks we want to get done. But there are little moments, too, down to a spare second here or there—waiting in line at the grocery store, driving the car to work, the last few moments of a lunch break.

I have talked to you about the tyranny of the urgent, but this is the kind of tip that helps you keep from becoming that robot. Use the *little* moments, the air in the mason jar, to make quick calls and check on friends, to pull out your goal sheet and see how you are doing, to say a quick prayer to reconnect with God.

It seems that the jar always has a little more room than you think.

FLEX THE LONG-TERM, FIX THE SHORT-TERM

Business gurus now tell us that it makes no sense to have ten-year goals. The world and the market are changing too fast in this global economy. Smart businesses are learning to *travel light*, creating plans that can be adapted on the fly.

We need to be the same way in our lives. I would advise you to be flexible in your long-term dreams but to have fixed short-term goals. I often tell young people to write their dreams on their hearts in pencil, not indelible ink. Times change, hearts change, we change. What happens when a young man or young woman graduates from college and sets a goal, say, of being a millionaire by the time he or she is thirty? For one thing, the goal cannot be absolutely controlled by the person pursuing it. In addition the goal doesn't take into account all kinds of things that can happen in the world and in the economy, such as the recession we have seen in recent years.

A good dream is, "I would like to open my own restaurant, and if possible I would like to open it before the year _____." It is focused, but it has some flexibility.

Meanwhile, you should be much more fixed with your short-term goals—the shorter they are, the more disciplined and stubborn you should be about sticking to them. Write down exactly what you want to get done this month, then this week, then today. That last one should be the most specific, the most attainable, and the most insistent. Do everything you can in your power to reach it because if you don't, you start tomorrow playing catch-up in your weekly and monthly goals. If you fall two days behind then perhaps three, you begin to be discouraged. Then when you don't hit your monthly goal, you hear yourself saying, "What's the use?"

Work a little bit of a fudge factor into your weekly goal and a more liberal helping of fudge into your monthly goal. Make your daily goal something you know you can do without killing yourself. But once you have set it, be sure you get it done.

Again, I truly believe that the key to time management is having a clear strategy and timetable up front. Once we have the map, we do a lot better job getting somewhere.

TRUST THE LORD OF TIME AND RELAX

Finally, chill out!

You might be surprised to hear me say that after talking so much about hitting goals. I just want you to know that it is not necessary to triple your stress level to be goal oriented. If you tense up, you are never going to make it.

When I went through my awful period of thinking my days on earth were nearly up, my priorities were rearranged. That is why you hear me talking about certain kinds of goals: reading my Bible cover to cover, spending more time with my family, keeping my body in shape. Do you see a theme there? Those are things that I consider highly important. Yes, I have business interests, and I am pursuing them vigorously. I have designed a new device for radical breakthroughs in exercise, and I am excited about marketing it in schools, in homes, and everywhere else. But I have made a distinction between what is significant and what is nonessential. The tyranny of the urgent will never rule my life again.

The truth is, my days are still numbered. So are yours. The Bible teaches that God knows when each sparrow will fall and how many hairs are on your head. He knows precisely how much time he has given us, so I *respect* time. I consider every second to be precious because it is a gift from God to me. But I know that it is a gift of love and grace, like everything else he has given us; it is not an ultimatum or threat. He has things he wants you and me to do, but the point is that we should get joy from doing them, and that through this joy he will be glorified.

So rest. Be at peace. The Lord of time will give you every moment you need, and he will give you the strength you need for every moment. Enjoy the gift.

"This is the day the LORD has made; we will rejoice and be glad in it" (Psalm 118:24).

12

Body: Sow in Health, Reap a Longer Life

Just going by statistics, you wouldn't call Orville Rogers a speed burner. He can run half a mile on a high school track in just over four minutes. But that is not bad for Orville's age, which is ninety-one years old.

Rogers was profiled in a recent article in *USA Today*. As someone nine years from his one hundredth birthday, he has every right to be satisfied with his time in the mile: just under 9:57. He claims the title as the world's fastest nonagenarian, and no one has stepped up to challenge him.[1]

How has he done it? Don't look for any shocking secrets. He says he eats healthy foods, runs ten to fourteen miles each week, and lifts weights regularly. I find this fascinating. Most of us live by the truism that our bodies just naturally fall apart as we grow older; we act as if that is just an unavoidable part of aging. As we get older, many of us relax, stop watching what we eat, and get no more exercise than walking to the car door and back, but we assume it is just the work of nature when our physical health begins to decline.

Yet I am over the age of sixty, and I can tell you I have every intention of running a mile or two, just like Orville, thirty years from now. Imagine running a footrace with your great-grandchildren. Isn't that a wonderful thought?

Don't get me wrong. Genetics does play a part in how we age. There are also diseases and other circumstances that are out of our control, and all of these things will have an impact on the level of health we are able to maintain. I'm just saying that it is incredibly foolish to pretend that we have no say in the matter. In most cases we are the ones who have the greatest control over the quality of life we can expect as we navigate the journey that lies ahead of us past sixty, seventy, or eighty years of age.

Luigi Ferrucci is director of the Baltimore Longitudinal Study of Aging at the National Institute on Aging. He directs research that has gone on for half a century, tracking people from youth through their elderly years, and he has some interesting conclusions.

For one thing, he finds that how you feel about aging at forty or fifty will say a lot about the quality of your life when you actually reach the golden years. In other words, if you have a negative attitude about growing older, you are going to be in worse health than if you enter with a positive attitude. Well, that supports a lot of other things we have said in this book. The people who age gracefully are somewhat of a contradiction because they have a positive attitude about it—yet they fight it.

"Those who fight aging age better than those who passively accept the decline that comes with it," Ferrucci says.[2] And how do you fight it? Obviously, you treat your body just as you would if you were twenty-five and preparing to run races, play tag football with your kids, and maybe get in several rounds of racquetball in between.

As a matter of fact, you don't even need to catch all the breaks in terms of health issues. Many high achievers among our seniors are people who have suffered through genuine setbacks, but they are resilient and determined not to let misfortune have the last word. Many people who have had knee or hip surgery, have survived cancer, or have experienced other medical problems become our shining examples of physical health later.

But the baby boomers, those born between the end of World War II and the early sixties, aren't necessarily showing signs of taking on aging with the energy you would expect from the Woodstock generation.

"Baby boomers expect a cure," says Laurie Jacobs, another scholar of genetics and aging. Their parents faced harder times and learned that being mentally tough is the key to survival, but baby boomers are used to reaching goals with their wallets—they think that a membership at the gym or a diet pill will be an instant fix. The problem here is that you can start going to the gym, but if you're not mentally tough, you'll never keep it up. You can take diet pills, but you have to push away from the table and eat healthier foods if you want a real solution.[3]

Mental toughness: that is a power base in itself. But it is not the one we will deal with specifically in this final chapter. I have saved the issue of health for last because we are talking about skills and touch points for a successful future. The future means more than next week—it is really the rest of your life, and that means that at some point you will face the issue of aging. And the very best way to prepare for aging is to care for the body God gave you.

You say you thought the answer would be more *spiritual*? I say, sure, but your spirit is always going to be affected by your body; we are holistic individuals. You say that mental or emotional issues are more important? Same answer.

In a way, your body is more than a power base. It is the ultimate one because it is your *home* base. Even if you have made quite a bit of money during your adult years, you can't buy a second body like you could buy a second home. There are no upgrades. If you don't care for your body, you will suffer mentally, spiritually, and emotionally.

So let's talk about your body.

A STATE OF DECLINE

I wish Orville Rogers, the ninety-one-year-old track star, was emblematic of where we are with the issues of health and fitness in this day and age. The truth is not so rosy.

As you have no doubt heard many times of late, we are growing more overweight every year. In the United States obesity has increased from 11.6 percent to more than 25 percent in the last two decades. That makes a total of fifty-five million Americans who are obese, and these people are at significant risk for other diseases, such as heart disease, diabetes, strokes, or cancer.[4]

And that brings us to another problem: the issue of the cost of caring for our health. Even simply as good citizens, shouldn't we be doing all that we can to care for the bodies we have so that we don't become burdens to our families, our struggling health care system, and, of course, ourselves?

People are cutting out doctor and dental appointments and not getting the physical examinations that might tend to spur them toward better care of their bodies. And just as alarming, they are not raising their children to be good physical custodians of their health. Consider these statistics from recent research:

- Today's children get less than fifteen minutes of vigorous activity daily.
- Today's children spend 20 percent of their waking hours watching television.
- Over the last twenty years obesity in children is up 36 percent, and superobesity in children is up 98 percent.
- The average child consumes at least twenty ounces of soft drinks each day.
- Fewer schools offer recess or physical education. Only 36 percent of students get physical education daily; another 36 percent get two days or fewer per week of physical education.
- In existing physical education classes only 27 percent of the time is devoted to motor activity.
- According to surveys, 90 percent of parents think their children are fit; however, only 33 percent of children are actually fit.[5]

It's clear that we are not setting a good example for our children. In addition, our schools are also letting us down. It is time we have a revolution in the area of health and fitness awareness. In the mid-sixties we saw a tremendous increase in efforts to educate our kids about physical fitness through President Kennedy's emphasis on the President's Council on Physical Fitness. But over the years other things have become more important within our culture. Certainly our schools have a full plate when it comes to challenges, but these days we can no longer count on them to provide leadership in this area.

Yet it seems these lessons should begin in the home. What do children see when they watch their parents? More often than not, Mom and Dad are living utterly sedentary lifestyles. Dad sits at a desk all day, then comes home and sits in the recliner and watches his favorite shows while he waits for pizza to be delivered for dinner.

Mom is more likely to be on the go, but she, too, is so busy (from either a career or a day of housework) that she has little time for organized exercise. Since there is less time to cook, the family eats plenty of fast food even though Mom and Dad know that through it all kinds of bad things are being invited into the body's delicate system.

If you feel that I am painting a gloomy picture of the state of things, let me give you one more number: *forty-two*. What does that quantity signify? It is the current ranking of the United States in life expectancy.[6] Yes, you read that right. Citizens of our prosperous, God-blessed nation will live shorter lives than people in forty-one other countries. We spend more on health care than any other country, and we have plenty of good doctors and facilities and medicines, tons of information about fitness, and enough good food to share with the world. Yet these are the results.

How did we let this happen? For the answer, look around you at other people. I hope you don't have to look in the mirror for the answer. Researchers attribute the statistic to the incredibly high obesity rate in America along with other factors.

We hope to go to heaven someday, but we shouldn't be trying to expedite the process! There is too much God has for us to do in this world. Therefore, we need to live not only longer lives but higher-quality, healthier lives.

Believe it or not the Bible has plenty to say about this subject. God doesn't just love you for your mind. Let's find out what he says about your body.

GOD'S HOME ADDRESS

It's interesting to find a clue to good health in the very first chapter of the Bible. "God said, 'Look, I have given you all the plants that have grain for seeds and all the trees whose fruits have seeds in them. They will be food for you'" (Genesis 1:29 NCV). We can begin right there. All the ingredients of healthy eating are found in the wonderful fruit and vegetables that God gave us to eat. (If you can't get all the fruits and vegetables that you need, go to my Web site listed at the end of this book and check out Juice Plus. It is an amazing product and has done wonders for me and thousands of others.) We also have meat for protein. All these foods are best in their more natural forms. (It actually takes a good bit of effort for us to do the things to our natural foods that make them unhealthy.)

Then in the New Testament we find this truth: the human body is God's second home.

> Or do you not know that your body is the temple of the Holy Spirit who is in you, whom you have from God, and you are not your own? For you were bought at a price; therefore glorify God in your body and in your spirit, which are God's. (1 Corinthians 6:19–20)

It is important to know what the word *temple* meant to the people reading this letter in the first century. Before the time of Christ the temple was the only place where the presence of God could normally be experienced. People traveled for days to Jerusalem because there was only one temple and that was the only place where sacrifices could be offered, forgiveness granted, and God truly worshipped. The Bible teaches that when we become believers in Christ, the Holy Spirit comes to live within our bodies. Thus, it has not that we are standing on holy ground—we *are* holy ground!

This is why Paul, the writer of the words above, was telling his readers to take care how they lived. However we treat our bodies is the way we are treating the house of God. When we eat junk food, we are bringing garbage through the door and into the sanctuary. When we fail to exercise and care for our bodies, we are letting the temple crumble from within.

Both the Old and New Testaments teach that the body is a beautiful creation of God—that we are made in his image. Enemies of Christianity, such as the early Gnostics, often taught that the body was evil and the spirit was good; therefore, it didn't matter how people treated their health. Eastern religions often stress the soul or the mind over the body and say very little about issues of health. But the Jewish and Christian faiths have always taught that people are holistic—consisting of mind, spirit, and body—and that these elements cannot be separated. We read, "You shall love the LORD your God with all your heart, with all your soul, and with all your strength" (Deuteronomy 6:5). Jesus then repeated this verse and said that it was the greatest commandment of all. If we are to love God with all of our strength, does it not stand to reason that we need to care for and enhance that strength?

Though the Bible mentions body, mind, and spirit, it never implies that these are separate things. The biblical idea is always that there is one person, and while he or she has these different aspects, they cannot be separated. It's interesting that in recent years science has finally caught up with what the Bible was saying all along. Doctors are beginning to understand what they call psychosomatic illnesses, which happen when issues of the mind affect the health of the body. We know that lonely people see their physical health deteriorate more rapidly, and that good marriages make for healthier husbands and wives as the partners grow older. It has been shown several times that people who pray are less prone to diseases of all kinds.

But this is a principle that works the other way too. Keep your body in good shape, and you are going to see your state of mind improve. It is true for many different reasons. For instance, if you get vigorous exercise, you will sleep better. There is a great deal of research to show that more people than ever before have sleep problems. We are sleeping fewer hours and getting lower-quality rest; this deficit affects the mind and the soul during our waking hours.

It is also true that physical exercise is one of the best ways to manage anxiety and stress. Next time you feel extremely tense or even a little low in spirits, take a vigorous walk. Push yourself and work up a bit of a sweat. For even better results take along a friend and talk about the issues that are bothering you. Both of these activities—exercise and fellowship—are healing in nature.

Think of it: *you are a temple of the Holy Spirit.*

In other words, you are God's second home; he has one in heaven and one on earth. We are heavenly real estate. When we care for that home, God is pleased, and we receive all the blessings that go along with good health: a stronger mind, more positive emotions, and the simple joy of feeling physically well.

THE POWER OF NOW

As I consult with people about these fitness issues, I find that every single one of these people has good intentions. I have yet to talk about fitness with an adult and hear that person say, "I'm not interested in taking care of my body. I just plan to let my health deteriorate over time."

I don't need to spend any more paragraphs convincing you that this is important. I would predict that all I really need to do is light a fire under you, right? You need an extra dose of inspiration and motivation—a sense of urgency that this is an issue in your life that simply cannot wait.

Let's start here. For every day that goes by, you are building a wall of bodily resistance that will be that much harder to bring down. In other words, it is much easier to lose five pounds than fifty. I have seen people set amazing goals for weight loss and meet them, but it never needed to be that difficult or to require that level of discipline; all they needed to do was apply smaller doses of discipline over time.

Many adults are gaining weight at a rate that isn't particularly notice-able from week to week, for example, two pounds per year. Two pounds isn't much—until the years pile up. At the end of ten years, the difference is twenty pounds. Then these folks happen to see old photographs of them-selves and react in horror. "Have I gained that much weight? When did *that* happen?"

One of the greatest powers I know is the power of *now*. We live in this moment—not a second in the past, not a second in the future. Sometimes procrastination becomes a vicious cycle. The more we put something off, the harder it is to take action. It can be a simple thing that we need to do, but it grows to the height of a giant that must be slain because we create a mental block over our refusal to do what needs to be done.

Make a list of the things you have been putting off: a dental checkup, cleaning the refrigerator, getting back to the gym. When you say, "I'm going to do this now," you empower yourself to take charge of your life rather than be the suffering slave of delay, constantly beating yourself up on the inside. If you haven't exercised for a while, start off slowly. Take a good walk, at an appropriate pace, to work up a good heart rate for your age and health status.

If walking is the best and most convenient thing you can do, stick with that for a while until you're inspired to do more.

The important thing is that you do something *now*. Let me tell you about a startling realization I had when at age fifty-nine I went back to play my senior year of football. I was able to do this because I had treated my body as a temple. Ever since I left school, got married, built a family, and navigated various careers, I had fed my passion for fitness. I knew I was in good enough shape to go for it.

Though I had lived with regret for three decades, when I got there, passed the physicals, and made the team, it occurred to me that I could have done this *years* ago! That's right—at any time from age twenty-two to fifty-nine, I could have done the thing I was doing now. Yes, the years pile up. It is amazing how much time can pass without us taking action on the issues that would make us healthier and stronger. I do believe it was in God's plan for me to come back when I did. He was glorified through the story as it reached a national audience through television and when it became a book. But that is something he has done *despite* me, not thanks to me.

The principle that springs from this idea is that what we sow in health, we reap in time. Sowing and reaping constitute an important theme in the Bible: your actions today create a legacy to your future. How many different ways can it be said? Eat it today, wear it tomorrow. Exercise today, sleep better tonight. Work out this year, enjoy greater health for years to come.

The ultimate power of *now* is a power over the future. We need to look at everything we do as seeds thrown into the soil of the future to bear some kind of fruit.

What investments in your future did you make today?

HALLMARKS OF HEALTH

Let's talk about the concepts that will help you adopt a better program of health and some that will simply get you hooked on good health forever. These come from my years of working in major college athletic programs in the areas of health and fitness. If you can master these simple ideas, you can take charge of your health and wellness and have more energy, better looks, and a longer life.

- *Faithfulness*. Have you ever started something and let it slide? Of course you have. I have already talked about my observations at the local gym. In January, the halls are crowded with eager adherents of New Year's resolutions. They come in with every intention of making a new start. But so many of them will fall away. In our sowing-and-reaping analogy, these intentions are like the seeds described by Jesus that never take root in the soil and are carried away by birds. Short-term diets and exercise programs actually discourage us because later we think, *Oh, I've tried that and found out I couldn't keep it up*. Nonsense! We keep up every activity we have established as a high priority. We need to be sure that the seeds take root. Build accountability into your life. Make a poster and mark off each day's progress. Have a workout partner and make a commitment to keep each other faithful. Faithfulness is the first and greatest test of any new change we want to make. Begin with the idea of a strong covenant before yourself and before God. You will see this thing through.
- *Discipline*. Discipline is based on the principle of deferred gratification. Bad habits are difficult to break because we don't like the pain and discomfort that occurs while we are changing the pattern. But a little effort now means a lot of satisfaction later. Olympic athletes work for years just to make the team and have the opportunity of one shot on the world stage. That one shot is the deferred gratification from thousands of hours of hard work and concentration. Discipline is good for the soul too. Once you have found you can gut it out and get something done, even when it hurts, you will believe you can do the same in other areas. If you can make it to the gym three or four times a week and persevere in your workouts, then turn that into a month, then a year, you will take pride in what you have proven about yourself, and you will apply it elsewhere. For example, you will be able to get up thirty minutes earlier in the

morning to read the Bible. If you can't do thirty minutes, then start with five; even if you are only reading a few lines, you will be better off than you were before. The point is to start. You will also find the will to push away from the table before those second helpings—hey, you have worked hard to sweat off those calories, so why put a hundred of them back in five minutes of eating? Discipline helps you see those issues with clarity. And you need to know going in that the benefits of discipline are seldom immediate, but they are guaranteed.

- *Embracing small victories.* I have found that everyone needs to feel the adrenaline surge of success each day, probably several times a day. You need that feeling of "Hey, I did something good!" In exercise, such as workouts with the Powerbase system I've developed, those victories are right there for you. It's great to take a few minutes, set a goal of repetitions for your exercise, and exceed what you did yesterday. It is even better to make a chart so you can see how far you have come over the months. Those small victories develop a healthy mind-set, and they keep you going on your exercise plan, your diet plan, or any other quest. A steady diet of small victories makes for a positive and energetic attitude in life.

- *Stress reduction.* It is a well-known fact that exercise is a wonderful way to combat stress. Some of the reasons are common sense. For example, physical exercise gives us a feeling of autonomy, of doing something rather than sitting passively. We are taking at least some action into our own hands. If I have a rough day but have still gotten to my workout, I feel as if this one thing has been productive in my day, and that takes an edge off of any low spirits I may have from other issues. I also know that exercise increases blood flow to my brain, and this releases hormones, stimulates my nervous system, and increases certain chemicals that work like natural morphine, enhancing a positive mood. This feeling is part of the runner's high you may have heard about. The adrenaline from exercise can also act as an antidepressant. We take so much medication these days even though God has placed many of the solutions in plain sight, right there for us in nature. I'm not taking a stand against your doctor's prescribed medication, by the way; I'm just saying there are other positive, natural things we can do that are good for the spirit.

- *The prayer factor.* Speaking of the spirit, here is a highly personal tip. I believe in prayer, and I also believe in the discipline of good exercise. When I put the two together, the results are incredible! Talk about a total body workout; you use your mind, soul, and strength all together, focusing them on God. You are a living model of Deuteronomy 6:5. This is great multitasking. We say we don't have time to read our Bibles or to pray. One of the great things about a workout is that it is not rocket science. It's recess period for the mind, so why not use it positively? While you are running or while you are on the bike or elliptical trainer, you can talk to God. You can listen to relaxing worship music on your MP3 player, and you can even memorize Scripture. By the time you leave your health facility or the place where you run or exercise, you will have benefited every part of your person. That will quickly become a daily power base for you.

- *Rebuild yourself.* A good strength-based workout overloads the muscles you are working. You tear your muscle tissues through the process of pushing them to their limit. That may sound like a bad thing, but believe me, it is not as long as you work out in a healthy way with guidance from a knowledgeable instructor. The next day you are going to be sore because those muscles need to rebuild themselves. It takes them a day or so, but when that happens, they are stronger than they were before. Think of someone who builds a wall, sees it overrun by the enemy, and builds it higher. God designed your muscles to keep rebuilding themselves to a tougher level each time you push them beyond their limit. This is a healthy process. If you are working with weights, you will note that you can do more repetitions and bear higher loads as the weeks go on. The more you tear down and rebuild your muscles, the more strength, power, and simple good health you will have in your body. But what happens when you don't work out? Your muscles begin to atrophy (shrink in size) within seventy-two hours of not being worked. They realize they aren't needed, and they become weaker. When you allow this, you will find that you have less energy and less endurance, and it becomes harder to do simple tasks.

- *Cardiovascular benefits.* Aerobics and other forms of cardiovascular exercise are good for your heart and your lungs. When you run, swim, cycle, or power walk at moderate levels of intensity, you exercise your heart in the way strength-training works out your muscles. In a healthy way you increase your heart rate so that more blood circulates through your system. Anaerobic and aerobic exercises reinforce the chest muscles you use for breathing and help your airflow. They make the heart muscle stronger, improving its pumping efficiency. They also strengthen muscles throughout the body as you get better circulation. As the total number of red blood cells improves, more oxygen is available to the parts of your body. As the muscles begin to increase their workload through greater anaerobic or aerobic activity, the body intensifies the number of red blood cells available to carry the additional oxygen needed to various areas of the body. And again, research has shown that exercise actually bolsters mental health. So you will have not only less anxiety but also be far less susceptible to heart disease and strokes.

- *Better relationships.* So what does a workout have to do with other people? It ultimately has a powerful effect, beginning with how it makes a person feel about himself. Many people today lack self-respect, and a common reason is that they don't like their appearance; they are unhappy with what they have allowed to happen to their bodies. Getting into a good workout regimen is taking action against that trend. We begin to feel better about ourselves, and we find that we are less insecure when relating to others. As we all know, we can't love others effectively until we know how to love ourselves. We also earn respect when people see what personal discipline is doing for our health. It is easy to become a role model, to stimulate someone else to take control of his health and wellness. This, of course, encourages us even more. As a matter of fact, many people find a whole new community of friends in a workout environment. Why? There is something about working together and sweating together that creates a bond between us. You find yourself looking forward to talking to that friend who is always on the other bike. It is also good to have an accountability partner who rides with you and works beside you. The shared exercise will make your friendship even stronger.

HOW TO LIVE LONGER

Are you still thinking about that declining life expectancy in America? Me too. It is very alarming.

But here's the good part: I can refuse to become a statistic, and so can you. I have decided to live as long as God allows me to remain on this earth, to serve him, and to care for my body and make those years as joyful and fruitful as possible.

In an article published in 2005, *National Geographic* identified three places where people are living significantly longer than those in the rest of the world. Those three spots are Okinawa; Sardinia; and Loma Linda, California. But there has been no systematic worldwide study of this—there could be other places. So researcher Dan Buettner decided to look around and see if he could find additional regions that seemed to have *fountains of youth*. He discovered the Nicoya Peninsula in Costa Rica, where it is quite common for people to live past ninety and even into their hundreds. He traveled there with a group to find out what these people were doing to extend their life expectancies.

Factor one, he found, was diet. Plenty of sun was another factor—this is why retirees often move to places such as Florida. Good water was another factor. These were all fairly obvious characteristics of a healthy environment—food, water, and plenty of sun, the very things you would want to give your potted palm. But Buettner looked a little deeper and found a few factors that were more compelling.

He discovered that the people of the Nicoya Peninsula have a particularly strong sense of purpose. "They felt needed," he said. "And they wanted to contribute to a greater good."

He found that there was a strong family dynamic in this region. People tended to remain close to their families, including the elders who were past the century mark. People in the family took good care of each other.

But they were also involved in strong neighborhood relationships. Perhaps it was a bit like the America of yesterday, small-town America, where people sat on their front porches in the evenings and visited one another rather than surfing the Internet or watching hours of television. The sense of community in the peninsula was very strong and characterized by laughter and listening.

Finally, Buettner believed that these were people who tended to find joy in their work. They weren't consumed by continually hunting for better jobs, navigating office politics, counting down the hours until the weekend, or any of the things we often do to make ourselves miserable from nine to five. These people were involved in manual labor and found it satisfying. They sensed that work is not a curse from God but a blessing given to help us express ourselves and be creative.[7]

Buettner's research gives us one last thought as we approach the end of this book. Folks in an obscure region of the world are finding a joy and sense of accomplishment that many of us crave though we have more money, more luxuries, and more of almost everything that ultimately doesn't matter. I find that so many of us today have lost touch with the things in life that truly satisfy: a good physical workout, whether at the nearby gymnasium or on a farm on the Nicoya Peninsula; a time of quiet reflection and prayer, in which to enjoy the silence and hear God; strong, committed relationships with other people; the joy of really nailing the fundamentals of our work; the focused pursuit of our dreams. These are some of the themes we have explored in this book about the power bases of life.

As we come to this final illustration, I would like you to see that our dreams need not involve wealth, fame, or power. The people of the Nicoya Peninsula probably wouldn't understand our complex conceptions of those things. But they have found the power bases of good relationships, healthy living, and rewarding labor, and they age very well as a result. When they pass on, they are surrounded by loving children, grandchildren, and great-grandchildren.

When my time comes, I plan to depart in the same way. But I believe I still have a great deal to accomplish before that. I am experiencing the joy of walking in God's will by doing the things that please him, especially serving other people. More than ever before, I feel that I am connected to the power bases I was meant to draw strength from as I try to live a fruitful and meaningful life.

I hope that this book has given you a few clues as to how you can do the same. I am curious. Which chapters did you find most compelling? Which concepts are you going to focus on putting to work first? I would love to hear from you. My home on the Web is www.mikeflynt.com. Stop by sometime and share your thoughts.

In the meantime, I hope you won't put this book away without acting on the ideas we have discussed. I don't claim to be the wisest man in the world, but I have lived a unique life, and the powerful truths I have found can bless you as they have blessed me.

I pray that you live the power-based life, that you will find meaning and purpose by drawing from the wonderful blessings that God has made available to us, whether through body, mind, or spirit. And someday when we are reunited in the world that lies beyond this one, we will experience together the greatest base of power in the universe.

Notes

Chapter 1   Power Base: Play to Your Strengths

1. Marcus Buckingham, *Now, Discover Your Strengths* (New York: Free Press, 2001).
2. Peter Drucker, *The Effective Executive* (New York: HarperCollins, 2006), 88.
3. Glen Van Ekeren, *Speaker's Sourcebook 2* (New York: Prentice-Hall, 1988), 7–8.
4. Phillip Brooks, *The Candle of the Lord and Other Sermons* (London: E. P. Dutton and Company, 1881), 299.
5. D. L. Moody, *To the Work! To the Work!* (Chicago: F. H. Revell, 1884), 87.

Chapter 2   Basics: Master the Essentials

1. Eric Zweig, *Gentlemen, This Is a Football* (Buffalo, NY: Firefly, 2006), 97.
2. Frederic H. Jones, *Tools for Teaching: Discipline, Instruction, Motivation* (Santa Cruz, CA: Fredric H. Jones & Associates, 2007), 89.
3. Vince Lombardi, *What It Takes to Be #1: Vince Lombardi on Leadership* (New York: McGraw-Hill, 2003), 137.
4. As a world-renowned author and success expert, Jim Rohn touched millions of lives during his forty-six-year career as a motivational speaker and messenger of positive life change. For more information on Jim and his popular personal achievement resources or to subscribe to the weekly *Jim Rohn Newsletter*, visit http://www.JimRohn.com.
5. Charles McGrath, "Most Valuable Player," *New York Times* Magazine, November 24, 1996; www.nytimes.com/1996/11/24/magazine/most-valuable-player.html?ref=charles_mcgrath.

Chapter 3   Mindscape: Cultivate a Winning Attitude

1. Viktor Frankl, *Man's Search for Meaning* (Boston: Beacon Press, 2006), 64.

2. James Allen, *As a Man Thinketh* (New York: Penguin, 2008), 13.

3. "Accentuate the Positive," music by Harold Arlen, lyrics by Johnny Mercer, ©1944.

Chapter 4   Visualization: See What Can Be

1. Robert Scaglione and William Cummins, *Karate of Okinawa: Building Warrior Spirit* (North Clarendon, VT: Tuttle Publishing, 1993).

2. R. J. Morgan, *Nelson's Complete Book of Stories, Illustrations, and Quotes*, electronic ed. (Nashville: Thomas Nelson, 2000), 548–49.

3. Nathanael Hawthorne, *The Great Stone Face* (Grand Rapids: William Eerdmans, 2006).

Chapter 5   Belief: Defy the Skeptics

1. Dr. James Dobson, *Hide or Seek* (Grand Rapids: Fleming Revell, 2001).

2. Nathaniel Branden, "Marriage Partnership," *Hope Health Letter*, March 1995, http://www.hopehealth.com/mab.asp.

Chapter 6   Commitment: Move Forward Relentlessly

1. Luciano Pavarotti, "Words to Grow On," *Guideposts*, March 1985.

Chapter 7   Team: Know Who You Play For

1. Ron Lieber and Rajiv M. Rao, "Zen and the Art of Teamwork," *Fortune*, December 25, 1995, 218.

2. Ibid.

3. "Accountability" entry, http://www.preachingtoday.com/illustrations (accessed February 24, 2010).

4. "Participation in the Sacrament of Reconciliation," *The CARA Report* (2009), 57–60, http://cara.georgetown.edu/bulletin/index.htm (accessed February 24, 2010).

5. *The Return of the King* (film), based on *The Return of the King* by J. R. R. Tolkien, directed by Peter Jackson, © 2001.

Chapter 9   Adversity: Turn Your Difficulties to Your Advantage

1. C. S. Lewis, *The Problem of Pain* (New York: HarperOne, 2001), 91.

2. The Quotations Page, http://www.quotationspage.com/quote/2771.html (accessed February 24, 2010).

3. Fanny Crosby, "All the Way My Savior Leads Me," © 1875.

Chapter 11   Time: Maximize Your Moments

1. Charles E. Hummel, *Tyranny of the Urgent* (Carol Stream, IL: Intervarsity, 2007).
2. Earl Nightingale, "The $25,000 Idea," Nightingale-Conant, http://www.nightingale.com/ae_article~i~206~article~the25000idea.aspx (accessed February 24, 2010).
3. Stephen Covey, *First Things First* (New York: Simon & Schuster, 1999), 88.

Chapter 12   Body: Sow in Health, Reap a Longer Life

1. Mary Brophy Marcus, "Healthy Lifestyle, Attitude Help Resilient Seniors Stay on Track," *USA Today*, November 9, 2009, http://www.usatoday.com/news/health/2009-11-09-Resilience09_ST_N.htm.
2. Ibid.
3. Mary Brophy Marcus, "How We Age: Lifestyle Key to Healthy Senior Years," *Daily Record*, November 17, 2009, http://www.zoominfo.com/people/Jacobs_Laurie_16012519.aspx (accessed February 24, 2010).
4. United Health Foundation statistics, cited in PR Newswire, "America's Health Rankings Show a Decline in the Overall Health of the Nation," November 5, 2007, http://www.prnewswire.com/news-releases/2007-americas-health-rankingstm-show-a-decline-in-the-overall-health-of-the-nation-58630812.html (accessed February 24, 2010).
5. Fitness for Youth, "Parent's Page," http://www.fitnessforyouth.umich.edu/frames/frameset_parents.html (accessed February 24, 2010).
6. Associated Press, "U.S. Ranks Just 42nd in Life Expectancy," MSNBC, August 11, 2007, http://www.msnbc.msn.com/id/20228552 (accessed February 24, 2010).
7. Dan Buettner, "Costa Rica Secrets to a Long Life," *AARP The Magazine*, May/June 2008, 69.

About the Author

Mike Flynt grew up in Odessa, Texas, and graduated from Permian High School in 1966. In 1965, he was first-team, all-district defensive back for the Odessa Permian Panthers' first state-championship football team; this team started the winning tradition at Permian and later inspired the book *Friday Night Lights*.

At age fifty-nine, with his final year of eligibility confirmed by the NCAA, Mike was able to make the football team at his alma mater, Sul Ross State University, and received national attention throughout the 2007 season, becoming the oldest contributing member of a college football team in NCAA history. Mike regularly played the last half of the season as linebacker and on special teams.

After completing his senior year of eligibility at Sul Ross, Mike returned to his responsibilities at Powerbase Fitness, LLC, where he continues to help people of all ages live a better, more productive life through strength training. Mike has been married to his beautiful wife, Eileen, for thirty-five years, and they have three wonderful children and two grandchildren.

Find out more about Mike at www.mikeflynt.com. You can contact Mike at mike@mikeflynt.com.

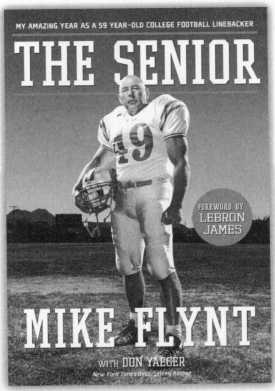